Romano-British Cavemen

Cave Use in Roman Britain

edited by

K. Branigan and M. J. Dearne

Oxbow Monograph 19
1992

Published by
Oxbow Books
Park End Place, Oxford OX1 1HN

ISBN 0 946897 43 3

Published and distributed by
Oxbow Books, Park End Place, Oxford OX1 1HN
(Phone: 0865-241249; Fax: 0865-794449)

Distributed in the United States of America by
The David Brown Book Company, PO Box 5605, Bloomington, IN 47407
(Phone: 812-331-0266; Fax: 812-331-0277)

*This work is published with aid of a grant from the
University of Sheffield Research Fund, and dedicated to
Mr J. G. Rutter in recognition of his painstaking
excavation of the Romano-British occupation of Minchin Hole, Gower.*

Printed in Great Britain by
The Short Run Press, Exeter

Contents

Introduction

This monograph is the result of a two year research programme conducted by the authors with the support of the Leverhulme Trust. The genesis and development of the programme are described in the first chapter. Chapter two discusses cave environments and their suitability for human occupation and usage, and then moves on to examine documented evidence of cave usage in Britain in historical and recent times. It concludes by discussing a series of temporal and functional models of cave usage against which the archaeological evidence of the Roman period might be set and tested. The third chapter then seeks to analyse in some detail the varying functions to which caves were put during the first four centuries AD. There is no attempt within these pages to argue the attribution of each individual cave to a particular functional or temporal model; that would be too repetitious. But examples of caves fulfilling each of the proposed functions are discussed to illustrate the testing of the archaeological evidence against the proposed models, and an appendix (2) lists the caves which we attribute to each functional group. In chapter four we examine the chronological and spatial distribution of cave usage, and discuss regional and chronological variations both of cave usage in general and of particular functions. The final chapter attempts to place cave usage in its wider context by examining the relationships between cave and open sites in both historical and socio-economic terms.

The book is completed by a summary gazetteer of the 97 caves we have identified as being utilised in some way during the Romano-British period, and by a list of 26 further caves for which a Romano-British usage has at some time been posited or suspected but for which we have found no reliable evidence. A full gazetteer with complete bibliography for each cave and a detailed description of the Romano-British assemblage from it, is being published as a separate volume (Branigan and Dearne 1991). The evidence for Romano-British usage of three caves (Thirst House, Wookey Hole and Minchin Hole) and for usage of the caves in Cheddar Gorge has been published and assessed in greater detail in four articles, but small quantities of important material from other caves previously unpublished or poorly published are published here in appendix 3.

In completing this programme of research we have inevitably relied on the help, advice and goodwill of many institutions and individuals and it is a pleasure to have the opportunity to record our gratitude. We are most grateful to the Leverhulme Trust, without whom the project could not have been undertaken, and to the British Academy and the University of Sheffield for support of a pilot scheme in advance of the main project. We owe much to the willing collaboration of the Keepers, Curators and other staff of the museums listed in appendix 1, and to the excavators of several of the caves, most notably Messrs D. Bramwell, E. Mason and J. Rutter. We are grateful for much helpful and expert advice to the members of our advisory committee – Dave Barrett, Mike Bishop, David Gilbertson, Clive Hart, Rogan Jenkinson and Ken Smith, and for specialist collaboration to Peter Smithson and Paul Nicholson. Finally we have to thank Russell Adams for so much advice, assistance and hard work on the final text. We hope the results of our programme justify their efforts.

1.   The Research Programme – Origins and Development

The author (KB) became interested in Romano-British cave usage when he was appointed to a lectureship in archaeology at the University of Bristol in 1966. Caves in the Mendips, Cheddar Gorge and at Wookey Hole were soon visited and the existence of some Roman material as well as prehistoric remains was noted. The activities of the University Spelaeological Society, and particularly its moving force, Professor E.A. Tratman, also made an impression of lasting significance. When, after ten years in Bristol, I moved to Sheffield in 1976 the importance of cave usage in Roman Britain was re-emphasised by the evidence from the caves in the Peak District and at Creswell Crags. Whereas in the south-west of England the role of cave usage in the overall pattern of Romano-British settlement was inevitably overshadowed by the wealth of other settlement sites, particularly towns and villas, in the Peak District cave usage assumed a much higher profile. Civilian settlement was (and fourteen years later remains) very poorly documented in this region, and in purely numerical terms cave sites represent perhaps a third of all known Romano-British civilian settlements.

A positive incentive to become involved in an assessment of Romano-British cave usage was offered first by Rogan Jenkinson and then by Mike Bishop. As chief ranger at Creswell Crags, Dr Jenkinson invited me in 1979 to examine and comment on the Romano-British material from various of the caves in the gorge. Subsequently Dr Bishop, Curator at the Buxton Museum, suggested that I might make a detailed study of the Romano-British metalwork from Poole's Cavern, in conjunction with analytical work on this material by Justine Bayley. This study was completed with the aid of a small grant from the British Academy and duly published (Branigan and Bayley 1989). It was during the research on this material, which involved also examining material from other Peak District caves, that the author became aware of the quality as well as the quantity of material from some of these caves and began to grapple with the problem of what this material represented in terms of Romano-British activity in these caves. A re-consideration of the evidence from the Mendips confirmed an emerging impression that cave usage was a significant part of the settlement pattern in both these areas, and that Romano-British use of caves in other parts of England and Wales would also be worth re-appraisal.

This conclusion was arrived at with some surprise because all the standard 'textbooks' on the archaeology of Roman Britain ignored cave usage altogether. The only, brief, exceptions were to be found in Frere's Britannia (1987, 266) and Todd's Coritani (1973, 102), as well as the author's own Roman Britain (1980, 218). Interestingly, all three of these authors warned against assuming that the cave users were impoverished peasants, but apart from that they were little more than passing references. In essence, the picture of Romano-British rural settlement was one in which small towns, villas, villages and farms all played a part but from which caves were effectively absent. The most recent books on Romano-British settlement and economy similarly ignore cave usage. Only in much more localised studies, often by local archaeologists, did cave occupation receive any recognition, and even then it was usually brief (e.g. Hart 1981, 105). It was therefore decided that the time was overdue for a thorough study of Romano-British cave usage in England and Wales.

The Research Objectives

The projected research programme was to have the following objectives.

1.   To produce a comprehensive catalogue of Romano-British assemblages from caves, which in addition to a record of the material found would also include a full bibliographical and archival record.
2.   To develop models for different cave usages (occupation, storage, industrial, funerary, ritual etc.) which could be tested archaeologically. This should involve consideration of ethnographic and historical information about cave usage.
3.   To seek evidence of cave environments in the Roman period, together with environmental evidence for seasonal or permanent usage of caves.
4.   To examine inter-site relationships between contemporary cave and open (i.e. non-cave) sites in the same areas.
5.   To integrate the results of the above to produce an interpretation of the usage to which caves were put in the Roman period, and to assess the significance of cave usage in terms of the overall settlement pattern in the same regions. The interpretation would extend beyond recognition of function to consider chronological and geographical variations of cave usage.

A proposal for a programme directed to these ends was placed before the Leverhulme Trust and the Trust generously offered a grant to cover a research programme to run from October 1988 to September 1990.

The Research Strategy

The first step taken on beginning the programme was to establish an advisory committee. We were fortunate that within easy travelling distance of the Department at Sheffield we were able to call on a wide range of expertise. David Gilbertson and Rogan Jenkinson advised on the environmental archaeology of caves, Mike Bishop on cave geology, and Clive Hart, Ken Smith and Dave Barrett on the cave and open site archaeology of the Peak District. In the early stages of the project, this committee provided invaluable advice as to what was possible and how it might best be achieved, and we were able to ask for further advice from the individual members of the committee throughout the period of the project.

Another immediate step was to initiate a questionnaire which was sent to over 40 museums, requesting information on any Romano-British material and associated archive from cave sites. Parallel with this, Martin Dearne began the literature search, and Keith Branigan the search for ethnographic and historical reports on cave usage.

It was also necessary to consider as early as possible the programme of environmental sampling and monitoring that might be needed, since monitoring would take many months of patient work, and analysis of samples could also be a protracted business. Given the expertise available to us, the accessibility of the caves, and their good range of Romano-British material, it made sense for environmental analysis and study to be focussed on caves within the Peak district and at Creswell Crags. Dr Peter Smithson agreed to mount a programme of environmental monitoring, the principal purpose of which would be to assess the suitability of a cave environment for seasonal and all-year-round occupation or usage.

Once the literature and museum search began to produce a catalogue of sites then museum visits, and whenever practicable site visits, were necessary. The museum visits were obviously designed to allow us to make as full an examination and record as possible of the relevant material in the collections, and to sift the archive for important and very often unpublished information. It was decided that where substantial unpublished assemblages were encountered, then we should try to undertake publication as soon as possible, to relieve our final gazetteer and catalogue of as much detailed description as possible. Site visits were important since location, accessibility, size and shape of caves were clearly crucial factors in the functions to which they could be put. There was surprisingly little information about these things in most archaeological reports on cave explorations, and cavers' manuals tended to concentrate on the deeper and archaeologically irrelevant parts of the caves.

Provision was also made from the start for the possibility of small-scale sampling excavation if it was thought that the right deposits were available in the right caves to provide either key environmental evidence or crucial stratigraphic documentation. Site visits therefore included assessment of the possibilities and practicalities of sample excavation.

It was intended that most of the identification and cataloguing of sites and assemblages should be completed within the first year of the programme, although late additions were expected. Site visits would take place over the first eighteen months, and any sampling excavations would be selected and undertaken in year 2 when the potential value of such work could be best assessed before it was begun. By the end of year 1 preliminary models of cave usage should be established, so that in year 2 they could be tested against the evidence accumulated in the catalogue. The other principal task of year 2 would be to devise and if possible implement ways of examining the relationship between cave and non-cave sites. It was envisaged that in addition to comparing the nature and profile of cultural assemblages from such sites we should also explore the possibilities offered by archaeometallurgy and ceramic thin-sectioning.

Publication would be at three levels. As mentioned above, substantial unpublished assemblages would be published as soon as reports could be prepared, and any results from environmental sampling and study would be communicated in papers to the appropriate specialist journal. A paper giving a summary of the main results of the programme would be prepared for publication in a national journal, and the detailed results and discussion, together with the gazetteer and catalogue would be published as a monograph.

The Programme as completed

The initial collection of data from museums and by literature search was accomplished with almost complete success. Only two museums failed to respond, but one of these unfortunately was the holder of the major collection of Romano-British material from caves in the north-west of England. The large and rich assemblages from the caves in the Settle area are held in private hands, and despite several attempts by letter and through intermediaries no response whatever was forthcoming from their owner. Given the importance of this material, the vast majority of which is unpublished, this can only be regarded as a highly unsatisfactory state of affairs. Certainly it has precluded our discussing these caves and their usage in any depth, although we do attempt in the catalogue and gazetteer to provide as complete a bibliographical guide and list of known material as possible. Miss Sonia Allen is studying these and other caves in the north of England and has had some access to material in private hands. We must hope this continues and that eventually this most important group of material is fully published.

In general, the amount of archive material in the museums was disappointing, as was the amount of faunal material that survived. The latter meant that we had to lower our expectations of evidence both for diet and for seasonal occupation. There was also, as we expected, the inevitable crop of 'lost' material. Nevertheless we have been able to catalogue a total of 97 caves and rock shelters in England and Wales that have produced Romano-British material; we have also been able to discount, for various reasons, another 26 caves which have previously been attributed a Romano-British phase of usage. The compilation of a detailed and accurate record of the assemblages from these 97 caves entailed visits to 17 museums. In the course of this we found important and largely or totally unpublished assemblages from Thirst House cave (Derbyshire), Wookey Hole (Somerset), and Minchin Hole (Gower), as well as important and badly documented material from the caves in Cheddar Gorge. We have prepared publications on each of these (Branigan and Dearne, forthcoming a–c).

Site visits proved a most valuable but also time consuming activity. Even with an eight figure map reference some caves proved impossible to discover in thickets and dense woodland; these were mostly caves noted as having small and well-hidden entrances. Nevertheless we managed to visit a total of 25 caves during the programme and in some cases the visits were crucial to an understanding of the way in which the caves might have been utilised in the past.

As we were well aware from the outset, many caves have been repeatedly used and continue to be used or explored today, so that disturbance of archaeological levels is widespread. Equally, the nature of cave environments and soil deposits is not well disposed towards the sort of environmental evidence we were hoping to utilise. In particular insect remains rarely survive in cave deposits. Our potential programme of environmental study was therefore somewhat curtailed, although Dr Smithson was able to carry out a full year's monitoring of the environment of Poole's Cavern. This cave was chosen for monitoring partly because of its accessibility from Sheffield, but also because it had produced a large Romano-British assemblage from controlled excavations and with a relatively low level of disturbance. Equally, the Romano-British material came from a restricted area in the cave, the environment of which could therefore be specifically monitored.

It was equally difficult to find cave sites where undisturbed deposits were in situ, accessible and likely to produce either useful stratigraphic evidence or environmental material. However, after discussion with members of the advisory committee, it was decided to excavate a small area within North Anston Cave. The cave was chosen because it might have undisturbed deposits, and in terms of size, accessibility and the nature of its Romano-British assemblage it appeared to be typical of a large group of caves apparently utilised for occasional episodic occupation. The opportunity to examine the nature of the deposits in such a cave was judged to be important enough to pursue. The most difficult, and in the end the most disappointing, aspects of the programme to follow through were the ethnographic and historical evidence for cave usage and the examination of relationships between cave and open sites. The documented examples of recent cave usage were for the most part thin on the sort of evidence in which we were particularly interested. They gave little detail of the interior furnishings of the caves and of the dispositions of material culture within them. They were also not very specific about episodic and seasonal use of the caves and the factors that affected these. In the end our models of cave usage were essentially theoretical with some occasional underpinning from observed practice. The problems of establishing the relationships between caves and open sites were complex and many, and are discussed in some detail in chapter five.

Publication of the results of the research programme has progressed largely as planned with one exception. We have noted above the papers on four specific assemblages, to which can be added specialist papers on environmental monitoring at Poole's Cavern (Smithson 1991, and Smithson and Branigan forthcoming), and Roman military metalwork from caves (Dearne 1990).

A summary article has been written and published in *Current Archaeology* (126, 248–50). This monograph represents the final element of the publication plan, but circumstances have necessitated the separation of the main report, discussion and gazetteer of sites from the complete catalogue of sites and archaeological material. The latter is now produced as a separate monograph, available for those institutions and individuals who want the full corpus of information (Branigan and Dearne 1991).

In summary, the programme has been completed as planned with the exception of the cave assemblages from the Settle area, and a more restricted discussion of cave-open site relationships than was originally hoped for. Nevertheless, we hope that the results reported in the pages which follow make a useful and new contribution both to the study of caves and to our understanding of settlement in Roman Britain.

2.   Cave Environments and Cave Usage

This chapter sets out first to examine the advantages and disadvantages of cave usage, moves on to look at the documentary evidence for cave usage in modern times, and finally seeks to establish a series of models both temporal and functional for the utilisation of caves.

In order to understand how caves were used, it first seems necessary to establish why they were used. In doing this it will be important to bear in mind the social and cultural context in which cave usage is being examined. Attitudes to cave usage must have been very different amongst stone age hunters and gatherers to what they were amongst farmers and craftsmen of the Romano-British period. The latter had the experience and the capability to build artificial shelters which could match the perceived attractions of caves in providing warm, rain and wind-proof accommodation, and could provide further comforts and facilities that could never be found within a cave system. In considering why Romano-British people should utilise caves at all we therefore have to bear in mind the alternatives they had available. They also had less need of the security provided by a cave since they lived in a landscape with few dangerous wild animals and under a political regime which had reduced inter-tribal warfare.

What are the attractions of caves for certain purposes, and how far do these attractions outweigh the disadvantages? At a superficial level one can easily list the possible attractions of caves. They can be warm in winter, cool in summer, they can provide shelter from heavy rains and strong winds, and they can often be easily defended from attack. Their less attractive aspects can be similarly listed – they are often cold, damp and dark and they cannot easily be kept clean. A superstitious people might also believe they were the haunt of spirits. But these of course are generalisations and they are little more than impressions. Equally to list the various characteristics of caves as pros and cons is simplistic: for some purposes a cold dark place, or a damp dark place might be thought ideal.

Before we can make judgements on such matters, however, we need first to try to establish more precisely the nature and characteristics of cave environments.

Temperature and Humidity

Most casual visitors to caves in Britain are immediately struck by the apparent cold and dampness of the cave interior. The difference in temperature is so noticeable because most casual visits are made in daytime and in good weather, which is most likely to be in summer. Caves cannot benefit from the direct warmth of the sun in the same way as open sites, and when they do warm up they do so very slowly; conversely they also lose heat very slowly so that at nightime the coldness of the cave is much less apparent. As for dampness, this too is unsurprising since most of the caves in Britain are found in limestone country where water percolates easily through the rock to emerge on ceilings and walls. Underground stream systems, which have often been responsible for creating the caves in the first instances, also flow in some caves. Monitoring of temperature and humidity in two caves utilised in the Romano-British period has provided more specific evidence of the fluctuations which might have been encountered by their users. At Robin Hood's Cave, Creswell Crags, July temperatures in the cave varied (in different parts of the cave) between 10°C and 13°C in contrast to a mean daytime external temperature of 24°C. In December internal temperatures varied between 4.5° near the entrance and 9° at the warmest place inside. There was no significant diurnal variation, in contrast to external temperatures which ranged from a daytime 6.2° to a nightime 3.8°. In winter, therefore, the cave was not only warmer than the outside but it did not suffer from the wide variations in temperature between night and day (Gentles and Smithson 1986, 210–11). In experimental use of fires in the cave, Gentles found that condensation very soon became a serious problem in the summer, and that on a summer's evening mist formed inside the cave. He noted that in December the cave was much drier and that condensation problems were reduced (Gentles 1984, 52–3).

At Poole's Cavern monitoring was carried out for a full year as part of this research project by Dr Peter Smithson (Smithson 1991). Thermistors were set up at nine points in the cave, including three on the terrace which was utilised in the Romano-British era. In August and September mean temperatures outside the cave were 14.5° and 13.3° in contrast to internal means at terrace point 6 of 7.2° and 7.2°. In November the external mean dropped dramatically to 7.2°, whilst the internal mean at terrace point 6 stayed at 7.2°. Thereafter, from December to April, the external mean varied between 4.7° and 5.5° whilst that at terrace point 6 remained stable at 6.6°. The coldness of the cave in summer was clearly demonstrated, but so too was its overall stability of temperature and its greater warmth in winter (Figure 2.1). As far as humidity is concerned, relative humidity was at, or close to, 100% throughout the year, and cave walls were constantly damp or even wet.

The studies at Robin Hood's Cave and Poole's Cavern, therefore, have demonstrated that at least for these two caves used in the Romano-British period, summer occupation can be relatively cold and damp and that in autumn and winter the caves offer warmer and certainly more stable and predictable environments. At Robin Hood's Cave, at least, condensation and humidity problems were less severe in winter.

Light and Heat

One of the most obvious requirements of cave occupation or usage is an adequate light source. Caves with large entrances or of only modest depth may be quite suitable for occupation or use as workshops, and equally caves which are to be used as temporary shelters or hideaways, or for burials or ritual, can be adequately lit for the brief periods of usage involved. If we find evidence, however, for caves which were occupied on a permanent or short-term (as opposed to seasonal or episodic) basis, and the evidence for such occupation or craft activity is deep in the cave or the cave has a restricted entrance, then the matter of light becomes an important consideration. So too does the provision of artificial heat if food preparation or craft activities are evidenced.

In the period with which we are concerned in this study (the first four centuries AD) the only sources of light were oil lamps, candles, burning torches, or fires. Equally the only sources of heat were fires fuelled by wood, charcoal, and (at least in Mendip) small quantities of coal. As sources of light for craft activity, oil lamps and candles would almost certainly have been inadequate and several burning torches or a substantial fire would have been necessary. Fires would also be necessary for the preparation of food, if not for heating. Experimental work conducted by D. Gentles in Robin Hood's Cave at Creswell Crags (Gentles 1984, Gentles and Smithson 1986) suggests that the use of fires in caves could be hazardous and should not simply be assumed to have been the norm in any cave under consideration (Figure 2.2). Gentles lit fires in July at two locations in the cave, one near the entrance and one towards the rear; the experiment was repeated in December, when external temperatures and internal air-flows might be expected to be different (Table 2.1). The results of these experimental lightings were as follows. In July, the fire at the entrance produced sufficient smoke to make the cave uncomfortable for use after about thirty minutes; only when the fire was reduced to embers did the smoke clear. The fire at the rear of the cave produced thick smoke which spread towards the entrance and made the cave unusable for about seven hours; in addition condensation around the fire became a problem. There was little improvement with the inner fire in December, but that near the entrance was a much reduced smoke hazard due to a different pattern of airflow. As Gentles summarised the results of his experiments "the value of the fire depends upon its location within the cave, its physical state and the time of year". It also depends, of course, on the shape and contours of the cave, the location and shape of the cave mouth and entrance, and on the outside climate and temperature.

In this sense every cave is unique, and without conducting similar experiments in all the caves with which our study is concerned it is not possible to say unequivocally that any particular cave could or could not have been lit, and heated, by a substantial fire. In general, however, it can certainly be said that occupants or users of caves would have had to take care and learn from experience as to which caves could be lit and heated by fires, where the fires could and could not be placed, what fuels could and could not be used on their fires, and lastly at what times of year a cave might be occupied and fires lit within it. In most cases one suspects that air movements were most favourable in the winter. It is possible that remains of substantial fires in a cave may point to winter usage (regardless of the need for heat), although one could not assume that usage of the cave was confined to the winter.

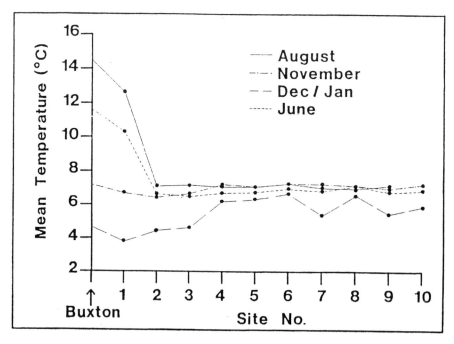

Figure 2.1   Monthly temperature variations at Buxton and at ten points in Poole's Cavern.

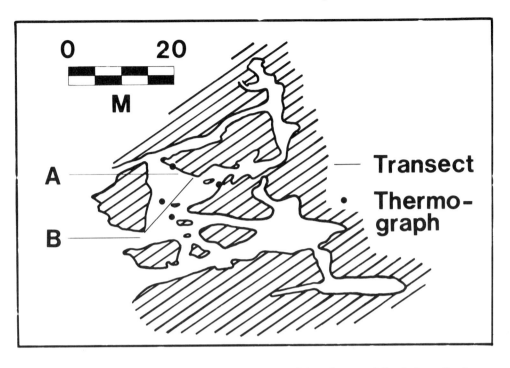

Figure 2.2 Robin Hood's Cave, Creswell, showing location of thermistors and Gentles' two fireplaces (a and b).

	Height above floor (m)	Afternoon		Night	
		a	b	a	b
	2.0	+2.8	+1.1	+3.8	+0.1
	1.5	+1.7	+1.1	+1.8	-0.4
JULY	1.0	+0.6	+1.0	+0.8	-0.4
	0.5	+0.1	+0.5	+0.2	-0.5
	0.25	+0.6	+0.8	+0.2	-0.2
	2.0	+3.5	+1.8	+3.3	-1.5
	1.5	+3.3	+2.1	+2.7	+1.5
DECEMBER	1.0	+2.9	+2.0	+2.4	+1.7
	0.5	+2.0	+2.1	+2.2	+2.1
	0.25	+1.5	+1.9	+1.9	+2.1

Table 2.2 Temperature variation at points a and b, Robin Hood's Cave, Creswell.

The crucial importance of these fires may well have been as much for lighting as heating, since Smithson's researches in various caves at Creswell (1982, 1986) and at Poole's Cavern (1991) suggests that the temperature in caves remains remarkably stable through the year and that it generally approximates to the mean annual temperature outside the cave. For heating purposes, if fires were needed at all then they could have been fed with embers. Similarly, ember-fed fires would have been suitable for cooking. Such fires, and those made with charcoal, would not produce sufficient light for craft work to be pursued however, nor perhaps in the further depths of the caves for normal living purposes. This is broadly the picture which Binford (1983) painted on the basis of ethnographic evidence, with sleeping and eating areas occuping the least well lit areas and production and craft areas situated near the entrance.

Security

For prehistoric peoples, particularly in earlier prehistory, the security offered by caves may have been a particular attraction, but as we noted above the threat from both human and animal predators was greatly reduced by the time of the Roman occupation of Britain. Such threat as remained would have come either from occasional brigandage or perhaps from raids by the Roman army itself should brigands or outlaws themselves choose to occupy caves. In these circumstances caves with obscure entrances in remote locations could provide welcome security, but where might such circumstances be found in the Romano-British period in England and Wales? Brigandage, rustling and other such activities are unlikely to have been a common feature of life in the Mendips and that is probably true also of the Peak District where the withdrawal of all the garrisons except that at Brough-on-Noe by the mid-second century suggests that the Roman administration considered the area pacified. The situation in north Wales and north Yorkshire is less easy to ascertain, since although forts were here throughout most of the Roman occupation these areas are more mountainous and much more difficult to patrol and control on a day-to-day basis. One might argue that the very presence of regular garrisons in these areas was required as much by local brigandage as by strategic considerations linked to the defence of the province's frontiers. If there was a continuing pattern of outlawry in these areas then caves might be used by either the outlaws or by their potential victims.

To summarise the pros and cons of cave usage it seems fair to say that by the Romano-British period many of the best reasons for occupying or utilising caves might seem to have been anachronisms. Strong, comfortable houses were commonplace in many parts of the province and threats from attack by either animal or human predators were probably less than at any previous period in Britain's history. On the other hand it must be allowed that some of the larger caves offered better living conditions than some of the stone and timber huts in which the farmers of the Pennines and Wales lived during the Roman occupation. We must also bear in mind the possibility that the predominant cave usage in the Romano-British period was not for occupation but for storage, occasional shelter, or for ritual purposes including burial. In all of these usages the so-called disadvantages of cave environments might either be irrelevant or positive benefits. What is undeniable is that the catalogue of caves with evidence of Romano-British usage is more than large enough for us to be certain that, for whatever reason, caves were utilised by the rural population on a significant scale. Some light may be thrown on this phenomenon by examining the evidence for cave use in modern times.

The Evidence of Recent Cave Utilisation

In trying to set up predictive models of different cave usage, it might be useful to first examine the documented evidence for cave usage in the recent past. In Britain cave usage continues to the present day, but principally for leisure purposes, either for exploration or as show caves. But cave occupation is well documented in the early twentieth century in the UK, and for security reasons, the Defence of the Realm Act of 1915 specifically forbade using caves as dwellings. Two years later a census of 'travellers' in Scotland recorded 55 persons still living in caves (C. Smith, forthcoming).

Permanent year-round occupation seems always to have been the exception rather than the rule, and in some cases at least is associated with people who were living at basic subsistence level and were little more than hunter-gatherers. Martin (1984, 123) records the occupation of a cave in Kintyre by Esther Houston and her son in the 1880's; the woman was described as an agricultural outworker, fisherwoman, and whelk-gatherer. Another example from Kintyre is also described by Martin (ibid.). Jenny MacCallum is said to have lived for half a century in a cave at Sunadale, making a living by hawking. She kept her various belongings in a sack; these included cooking utensils and various foodstuffs. She also kept a hoard of money (weighing 11lbs) in a bag. Another example of female occupation of a cave was described in Devon in 1878. In this case a small cave near Seton was occupied for 30 years by two women who were shell-fish gatherers (Kempe 1988, 149). A more recent example was documented in the Scottish Sunday Express (April 10, 1983) which recorded the thirty-year long occupation of a cave near Ballantree in Ayrshire by a single man who gathered wood from the beach and dead animals from the road. A similar occupation lasting thirteen years is recorded in the caves at Caiplie in Fife (Leitch 1987, 16–7) and here there are useful indications of the furnishings in such a cave. This cave-dweller put linoleum and carpets on the floor, and had a bed, table and chairs as well as a stove! The cave also had a door fitted to its entrance.

Permanent occupation of caves by farmers, however, is well documented in France and continues, albeit in most cases today in artificial caves hollowed from the rock. Permanent occupation of caves by industrial workers is recorded in Sandstone caves around Retford in Notts, and in artificially created caves carved from the ash and rock spoil heaps by lime workers around Buxton (Kempe 1988, 144).

Cave occupation is frequently associated with craft activity, and in particular with metalworking. Tinkers/tinsmiths are recorded living with families in Kiel Cave, Kintyre and at Wick in Caithness (Census Return 1881; Kempe 1988 141), and Smith (1986, 6) is surely correct in suggesting that the Tinklers Cave at Lochgilphead (Argyll) takes its name from its use by tinkers. In some cases the term tinkers was almost certainly used as a general description of families and individuals who had no fixed abode, other than perhaps a cave; it did not necessarily imply that these people were tinsmiths or blacksmiths. In the case of Kiel Cave, it is recorded that a basket maker lived in the cave alongside the tinker, whilst at Peak Cavern, Castleton (Derbys) a group of rope makers occupied the great entrance chamber of the cave. Thomas Kendrick is recorded as utilising the cave (now named after him) on Great Orme, North Wales, as a workshop in the the later 19th century, and although he had been a copper miner by profession the cave workshop was probably for stone working rather than metalsmithing (Davies 1983, 46).

In the case of Peak Cavern, a row of small terraced houses were constructed actually within the cave entrance, but this is unusual and was possible at Peak Cavern due to the sheer size of the entrance. Many of the cave-homes still occupied in France, and those previously occupied in the English Midlands, have however been extensively adapted and furnished to provide accommodation not very different to that found in contemporary houses. There is nothing to suggest such major modifications were common in earlier periods and the evidence of these caves is probably of little help to our study. But what little is recorded of the furnishings and living space utilised in the unmodified caves occupied into the early twentieth century in Scotland and Wales is potentially of greater interest. In Upper Kendricks Cave for example, an internal partition wall was constructed, and window glass and fragments of a wooden frame were also discovered, as well as general domestic rubbish and pieces of coal. With an area of about 11m x 8m, and an entrance about 3m wide, the cave provided a sizeable living or working area adajacent to a light source. The caves at Wick featured stone beds covered with matting, grass and bracken and were heated by numerous peat fires. Smith (pers. comm.) records traces of bedding, screens, windbreaks and 'ubiquitous' hearths from caves with remains of recent occupation in Argyll. In terms of size, the caves at Wick are 3m or more high and around 20m deep. The social groups using these caves vary from single families (or even individuals) to groups of several families in large caves. Smith notes that four is a frequently recurring figure, suggesting a cave population of perhaps 10–20 persons. In caves with multiple family occupation it was usual for each family to have its own hearth.

Temporary occupation of caves, sometimes specifically seasonal, is recorded by Smith. Ellary Boulder Cave, adjacent to the old road to Kilmory, he suggests was used intermittently as a shelter by travellers (Smith 1988, 4), whilst the tinkers' usage of Lochgilphead he believes must also have been no more than occasional (1986, 7). A cave examined in 1956 (Sanderson 1957, 243–5) was also an occasional shelter for packmen and other travellers and had minimal furnishings provided – a rough wall to protect the entrance, and rough screening of sacking erected on three wooden posts around a sleeping space. Smith also records (pers. comm.) that fishermen from Colonsay regularly stayed in caves on the west coast of Jura while fishing inshore waters, and a similar pattern may be behind the observation of Thomas Pennant in 1772 that St Ciaran's Cave was used by 'sailors' for cooking their meals. Further south, Kempe (1988, 145) records that caves around Mansfield (Notts) were used by 'nomadic' makers of besom brooms, which they made from heather gathered on the moors. There is little recorded of the interiors of these caves, but at Lochgilphead Smith (1986, 7) records rough paving and a series of rather structureless hearths.

The use of caves as fugitive lairs or hideaways, a rather special form of domestic occupation, is also well attested. Indeed there is a long tradition of such usage in Scotland from Robert the Bruce, Sawny Bean and Rob Roy, to Bonnie Prince Charlie. Where such usage is documented (and that is not always the case) the caves used tend to be in remote and inaccessible locations, such as Princes Cave on the east coast of South Uist, and/or have small, disguised entrances. Balnamoon's Cave in Angus, also associated with fugitives from the '45, is both remote and well disguised and its only furnishing was apparently heather bedding material (Leitch 1987, 17–9). Less celebrated fugitives, such as poachers are frequently associated with occupation of caves; Martin (1984, 125) records an example in 1894 in Kintyre, and tradition associates Soldiers Hole at Cheddar with a poacher (although here again it has also been associated with political fugitives, in this case from the defeat of Monmouths rebellion).

Finally we might note the use of caves for places of ritual, which in recent times has usually meant the location of Christian chapels. They are known at several places in France, and there is an example at East Retford with a chapel which is mentioned in Domesday Book (Kempe 1988, 145). Leitch (1987, 16) describes caves in Sutherland and Wester Ross which were used as places of worship as late as the 19th century, although the only furnishings he mentions are some benches in the cave at Ledaig. I have seen Chinese and Buddhist shrines in caves in Thailand. In all cases there is some modification of the cave and its entrance, and ritual furnishings are present in the cave and often immediately outside it. Further back in time, but documented, is the ritual usage of caves such as the Dictaean Cave in Crete, thought by the Greeks to be the birth place of Zeus.

Two potential usages of caves which are not well documented in recent times are as storage spaces (although caves are used for this purpose in Italy, and were extensively used as munitions dumps during World War II) and as places of burial. Finally, rock shelters and caves are certainly used as temporary animal pens in Mediterranean countries, and often have simple closing walls built across or around the entrance in order to keep the animals inside. Since the shepherds often stay in the same shelter, small hearths and scatters of occupation debris are to be found. There are in fact several documented examples of caves being similarly used in Scotland (Leitch 1987, 15; Edward 1793, 39; Shaw 1882, 62).

It is regrettable that there is so little documentation of what these various types of cave usage look like, in terms of the material remains associated with them, and useful as they are to confirm that caves can be utilised for a wide variety of purposes, it appears that our predictive theoretical models can be developed without undue attention to modern analogies.

Models of Cave Usage

In order to give better definition to the identification of the varying functions of cave usage in the Roman period, it was decided to establish a series of theoretical models of cave usage which could be used to assess cave assemblages. Where possible these models have been tested against documented cave usage of recent times, but most records of cave usage prove woefully inadequate in their detailed description of the cave itself and of the material culture associated with the usage. In developing these models particular attention has been given to material evidence of usage which might be expected to survive in an archaeological context.

It was recognised at an early stage that two overlapping sets of models would have to be developed, these being temporal models and functional models. That is, two caves serving the same function might yield different material evidence of usage if the temporal character of the two occupations differed.

Temporal models

It is suggested that the temporal character of a cave's usage might fall into one of three types – long-term, short-term, and episodic.

Long-term usage

A cave is occupied more or less permanently over a period of many years, notionally at least five, but very probably many more. The size, shape and location of the cave are likely to be well suited to its particular function. The quantity of artifact material from a cave in long-term usage should be relatively high if only because there are many more opportunities for loss and breakage of material. The material should reveal a broad chronological continuity over a prolonged period of usage. In so far as is identifiable, material evidence should also reveal usage at all seasons of the year.

Short-term usage

A cave is occupied more or less permanently over a period of at least one year but perhaps no more than five. The size, shape and location of the cave may not be ideally suited to its usage, but may be tolerable for a short period; their unsuitability may become a reason for occupation being only short-term. The quantity of artifact material is likely to be lower by reason of a short period of 'loss/breakage' opportunity. It should, nevertheless, reflect continuity over the period of occupation and one would expect no evidence of seasonality. It must be recognised that even in the Roman period it is in fact impossible to identify continuity of occupation over as short a period as five years from the chronological identification of artifact material.

Episodic usage

A cave is used only at certain limited times of year, possibly a specific season, although the occupation or usage may be repeated for many years. The size and shape of the cave may not be crucial to the function, but repeated seasonal use is more likely to be associated with caves that are of preferred size and location for that particular usage. Location may be important in that the cave may well need to be convenient in terms of the principal seasonal activities for which it is acting as a base. Artifact material may reveal the discontinuous nature of occupation, but if seasonal use extends over many years may be quite prolific. Environmental evidence might reveal evidence of seasonality.

Functional models

We suggest that the variety of functions fulfilled by caves may be represented by seven functional models.

Domestic occupation

The cave will be located near a water supply and probably close to either arable or pasture land, although this may not be essential in some instances. The cave itself should have a high ceiling in the occupation area since the lighting of fires to provide light and heat will likely create severe smoke problems (Gentles and Smithson 1986). The artifact assemblage from the cave should include a wide range of domestic debris – personal belongings and trinkets, a variety of unspecialised tools, and a varied pottery assemblage. This should include 'tableware', storage vessels and kitchenware. Food debris should also be expected.

Workshop occupation

It is recognised that caves used as workshops may also have been used as homes by the craftsmen and their families, and that the artifact assemblage may therefore include domestic occupation material as outlined above as well as material associated with craft activity. The cave is likely to be located near both woodland and water, since both wood and water are used in many craft activities quite apart from any requirement for domestic use. Craft activity will also need adequate light and space, and if fires are involved in the activities then there will be a need for high roof space, near the entrance. The key artifact evidence for craft usage will include specialist tools, raw materials, waste products, unfinished products, specialist vessels (crucibles, moulds) and possible specialist structures (furnaces, ovens, working-floors or surfaces). This material may be spatially discrete, if the archaeological deposits are undisturbed.

Shelter

In the Roman period, a cave used for shelter from the weather is likely to be at some distance from the contemporary base site of those who use the cave. It will have no special features of shape or size. The artifact assemblage will be restricted in both quantity and range, but since such shelter caves may have been regularly if episodically used, their users may have accumulated small quantities of domestic pottery in them and one might expect evidence of hearths and of food debris.

Storage

A cave used for storage may be particularly difficult to identify. It is likely to be near to an adjacent contemporary domestic occupation site, and with easy access. For storage of crops, fodder, and wood it should be dry, and a narrow entrance, easily blocked, might be preferred. Artifact material might be extremely scarce since the amount of time spent in the cave by its users would be low. There would be few opportunities for ceramic vessels to accumulate; more likely is the personal belonging accidentally dropped during the delivery or collection of stored materials.

Hideaway

In the Roman period the use of caves as hideaway places of refuge is likely to have been restricted entirely to those engaged in some form of illegal activity. Such caves might therefore be expected in remote and inaccessible places, and to be small in size with obscured entrances. Such caves are unlikely, by reason of their unsuitability, to have been occupied for any length of time. The amount of artifact material to be recovered from them is therefore likely to be very small, but to include some domestic pottery (with cooking vessels).

   Evidence for illegal activity is unlikely to be preserved but weaponry or counterfeiting materials might remain. A variation of the hideaway model would be the use of a similarly obscure cave for the hiding of wealth. In this instance, if it was not recovered, a 'hoard' might be expected if the wealth was in the form of coinage or metal products. There would be little if any other artifact material, however, and a cave used as a hideaway for wealth might therefore offer no evidence for usage at all if the material was recovered by its owner.

Shrine

There is no reason to think that use of a cave for ritual purposes is restricted to caves of any particular size, shape or location, although it was noted in discussion of modern cave usage that caves used as shrines have often been modified in some way, particularly at or near the entrance. There may be unusual rock formations, often stalactites or staligmites, which have formed the focus of some of the ritual. Artifact assemblages may include distinctively votive material (miniatures or 'representative' items made of thin sheet metal, or figurines), but they may also be expected to include other items which are normally found in domestic deposits. In a Roman or Romano-Celtic context these could include coins and jewellery. Separation of domestic from ritual usage might therefore present some difficulties. It is suggested that domestic usage should be a preferred identification unless there is evidence for modification of the cave and/or its entrance, a focus of artifact material around unusual rock formations, clear votive material, or a pronounced imbalance in the relative quantities of personal belongings. In the latter we would include excessive quantities of jewellery or coinage, relative to the quantities of ceramics, and an absence of tools or domestic implements.

Burial place

Caves used for burials might be expected to be either in a secluded location or else the burials within the cave may be located in its deeper reaches. The cave may well be unsuitable for domestic occupation by reason of its shape and dimensions. It will need to have a reasonable depth of soil at the point where burials are to be made. The key evidence will obviously be human skeletal material. Given the repeated use of caves throughout later periods, these may well be badly disturbed in most cases. In the Roman period one would expect low quantities of ceramics, possibly small numbers of coins, items of personal jewellery and possibly clothing appendages (buckles, clothing loops, boot nails). Traces of ironwork from coffins is possible but on balance unlikely.

All of these functional models may overlap with any of the three temporal models, except for the Shelter and Hideaway models. One would not expect these to be other than episodic usages. The Models are summarised in Table 2.2.

Table 2.2   Models of Cave Usage: A tabulation

TEMPORAL	Artifacts	Cave size/location	Environmental Evidence
PERMANENT USE	High quantity; chronological continuity.	Important to the function.	Evidence for occupation in all seasons.
EPISODIC	Low quantity; chronological discontinuity. Possible pointers to seasonality.	Less important to the function	Evidence for seasonality

FUNCTIONAL	Artifacts	Cave size and shape	Cave location
DOMESTIC OCCUPATION	Cooking, storage and eating vessels; food debris; wide range of other artifacts.	Standing height; dry and reasonably even floor surface.	Near pasture/arable/ water
WORKSHOP	Tools/moulds/waste/ raw materials, unfinished or multiple products	Standing height; natural or artificial light source.	Near wood and water.
STORE	No domestic material (esp cooking)	Not too deep	Accessible
SHELTER	Few and random; food debris, but few cooking and storage vessels.	No requirements	At a distance from base site.
HIDEAWAY	Small quantity of domestic material; possible wealth.	Small entrance, well concealed.	Difficult of access and/or remote
SHRINE	Absence of domestic assemblage; unusual groups/clusters of items, votives etc.	Maybe unusual rock formations	No requirements.
BURIAL	Human bones; personal jewellery; may be low amounts of pottery.	Possibly a deep cave; some depth of soil.	No requirements.

3.   Romano-British Cave Usage – Functional Analysis

In this chapter we seek to use the models and criteria of varying cave functions which have been discussed in chapter two to identify the usage of individual caves in the Romano-British period. We do not attempt to provide a cave-by-cave discussion of function, nor do we provide a justification of each and every attribution. Rather we discuss the general characteristics of each functional grouping and then look in more detail at those caves which provide the most reliable evidence of usage.

It has to be said at the outset that the evidence is uneven in quality and that in general it is unsatisfactory for a number of reasons. Some of the evidence available cannot be taken into consideration because it cannot be confidently identified as of Roman date. Many caves have been used in both the pre- and post-Roman eras and lack either stratigraphic or excavational separation of the debris from these different episodes of use. In this case material such as faunal samples, human skeletal material, and many simple items of stone, bone, iron and bronze cannot be assumed to be Roman and have to be excluded from the discussion. In many cases, the amount of recovered or surviving material is very small and has been recovered by chance or in small, haphazard soundings. In such instances the risks of biased samples makes attribution of function hazardous, although the location, shape and size of the cave may help to eliminate some possibilities.

In addition to these 'sampling' problems there are also the problems raised by the likelihood of a cave undergoing different usages at different times within the Roman period and the Roman assemblage itself being 'mixed'. Many caves, for example, must have been used as occasional shelters regardless of more regular or longer-term uses for burial or domestic occupation. A further complication arises where caves fulfilled two different functions at one and the same time. These may be spatially varied, as we shall see in Wookey Hole in the fourth century AD where occupation took place in one part of a cave and burial in another, or they may be complementary activities which took place in one and the same area. The most obvious example of this is the cave which is used both as a workshop and as a home, as we believe to be the case at Poole's Cavern. For all these reasons, the attribution of caves to one usage or another must be regarded as open to revision in the light of future discoveries and many attributions must be regarded as tentative. Where caves have more than one major function, whether contemporaneously or successively, then both usages are considered below and are cross-referenced in the summary list. Both usages are also taken into account where we refer to the number of caves used for a particular purpose (e.g. Wookey Hole is counted as both a domestic occupation site and a cemetery).

Since our prime concern here is with function, temporal variations in usage other than those directly related to function (shelters and hideaways are by nature episodic in usage) are not given priority of attention. We do however address the problem of temporal variations in so far as the nature of the archaeological evidence allows it.

Domestic Occupation

We reserve the term 'domestic occupation' for cave usage which involved all the usual domestic functions normally associated with living in a house. It does not include use of caves for temporary shelter or security (which we categorise as Shelter usage and Hideaway usage), but it may include either long-term or short-term occupation, and it may also include episodic usage if the cave is used on a regular but seasonal basis.

We identify twenty caves as serving as places of domestic occupation, six of which seem also to have served as workshops, and three as cemeteries. All of these caves meet the criteria proposed in terms of the cave location and size, and the 'domestic' nature of the assemblages, which includes table and kitchen ware, a variety of personal adornments, domestic tools such as knives and cleavers, and implements like rubbers and hones. Faunal samples were recovered from many of these caves and included the usual domesticates and in some cases deer, but the majority of samples could not be isolated as exclusively Roman. The Romano-British deposits at Albert Cave, however, produced a large faunal assemblage (almost entirely lost) which included according to Dawkins (1874) abundant ox, goat (and presumably sheep), and pig, but only a few bones of deer or wild fowl. The domestic character of these cave usages is also suggested by the occurrence at nine of these sites of spears and arrowheads, presumably used for hunting, and at five others of various farming implements. The only caves which have produced finds of either type are to be found in the twenty selected on other criteria as domestic sites.

There is regrettably little information about how the majority of these caves were actually occupied; hearths and concentrations of charcoal are mentioned in several accounts, often outside or near the entrance of the cave, suggesting cooking and any craft activity may have taken place there and that the inner areas were reserved mainly for sleeping. There is little or no direct evidence for furnishings or artificial modification of the caves, but seven caves attributed a domestic usage have produced large keys or latch-lifters suggestive of doors. It is of course possible that the doors were elsewhere, and the keys simply lost here but the latch-lifters are less likely to have been carried in the pocket. Equally, the fact that seven of the twenty 'domestic' caves have produced these finds whilst none have come from our other eighty caves does suggest they really belong here. That being so, one wonders what other timber modifications may have been made which have left no evidence. One suspects also that the iron strappings, bindings, studs, and nails which occur in some of these caves came from moveable furnishings.

As examples of domestic cave occupation, with no major workshop aspect, we may cite Elderbush Cave (P14) and Thors Cave (P29). At Elderbush the occupation area seems to have been concentrated near the entrance, with hearths probably in the open, possibly because although the cave was wide and deep enough for occupation, its ceiling in the Roman period may have been too low for general occupation rather than for a sleeping area. The pottery corpus includes jars and bowls in coarse ware and a handful of samian table vessels. Trinkets included a fibula, a pin and a ring, and tools included a knife and various rubbers, hones, and pot boilers. A small faunal assemblage from 'the Romano-British layer' contained mainly sheep/goat but some pig and cattle as well as deer. Thors Cave is a good cave for occupation, with a large main entrance passage and a subsidiary entrance which provides light. The main chamber is flat-floored and has a high ceiling, and here and in the entrance passage there were traces of hearths. Little is known of the pottery assemblage except that it was substantial. Personal trinkets were mainly fibulae and pins, whilst tools included knives and axes, pounders and hones. There were also fragments of two querns, and much faunal material (regrettably unidentified). This looks like the classic domestic assemblage.

With all of these domestic occupations we face difficulties in identifying the temporal nature of occupation. The archaeological evidence does not have sufficient chronological precision to allow the distinction between occupation over a period of three or four years and ten or twenty

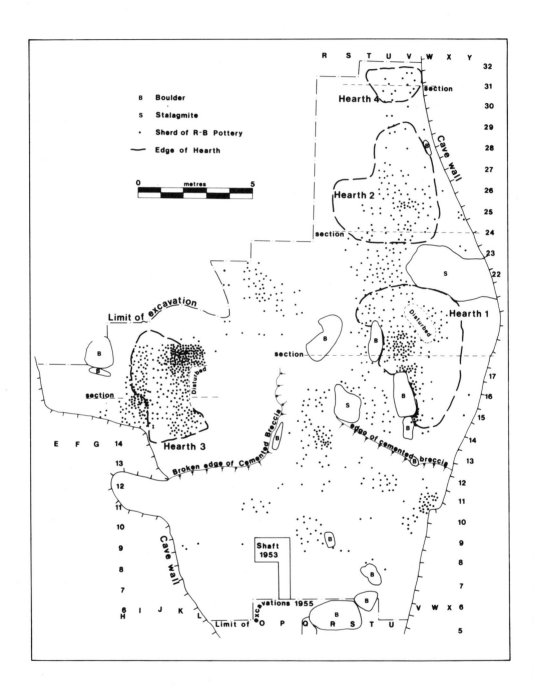

Figure 3.1   Minchin Hole, Gower, showing location of hearth areas and Roman pottery.

years (that is, between short-term and long-term occupation). Due to the nature of cave environments and the disturbed nature of most cave deposits, evidence of seasonal occupation is also difficult or impossible to obtain. All of the caves categorised as domestic occupation by us have produced sufficiently large assemblages to suggest prolonged occupation. It is also noticeable that of the seventeen such caves which have produced dating evidence of fair to good quality (see chapter four), eleven suggest 'continuous' occupation of a century or more and the other three of almost a century.

We recognise that there is no guarantee or even likelihood that occupation was literally continuous over that length of time, or that an assemblage dated as 'late first century to late second century' actually stretched over more or less a full century, as opposed to a minimal period of perhaps fifty to sixty years within those brackets.

Nevertheless, the quantity and range of the material evidence from these caves is in almost every case such as to suggest long-term rather than short-term occupation (as defined in chapter 2, supra pp.16–17). The recorded stratification at Thors Cave might be thought to support this view. Here it was noted that in the main chamber three deposits with much charcoal and each of about 0.3m depth overlay one another and were separated by layers of clay, also about 0.3m thick. All three layers seem likely to be Romano-British in date. This still leaves open the possibility that some or all of these domestic occupations were in fact episodic, specifically seasonal, occupations. Attempts to resolve this by recovering insect fauna from undisturbed Romano-British deposits in Poole's Cavern served only to confirm that such fauna do not often survive in British cave climates. At present we cannot resolve this problem and it must remain a possibility that some of our domestic cave occupations were regular seasonal ones, most probably in winter, over a prolonged period and associated with occupation of open air sites. We shall have to return to this scenario in chapter five.

The population of caves in domestic occupation is unlikely in perhaps the majority of cases to have been more than a nuclear family, since the usable areas of the caves are frequently too small to have provided sufficient space for a larger group. Indications that larger groups may have been involved in some caves are perhaps provided at Minchin Hole and Wookey Hole. The four 'hearth areas' at Minchin Hole recall Smith's observation (supra p.14) that recent domestic occupation of caves in Scotland is often associated with four families, each of whom had their own hearth (Figure 3.1). In the case of Minchin it has been argued that the distribution of material around the hearths suggests that at least one, and possibly two, were not major focuses of activity (Branigan, Dearne and Rutter, forthcoming). It remains likely that two family groups may have occupied this cave at the same time, and possibly as many as three. In the case of Wookey Hole, the only guide to the size of the population group using the cave in the fourth century is the contemporary cemetery in chamber 4. The minimum number of individuals buried here was 28 (Figure 3.2), and almost certainly some if not most of the 19 individuals whose remains were recovered from the stream were also originally buried in chamber 4 (Hawkes, Rogers, and Tratman 1978; Branigan and Dearne, forthcoming a.) The number of fourth century burials was probably in excess of 40, which should represent a contributing population of at least two nuclear families.

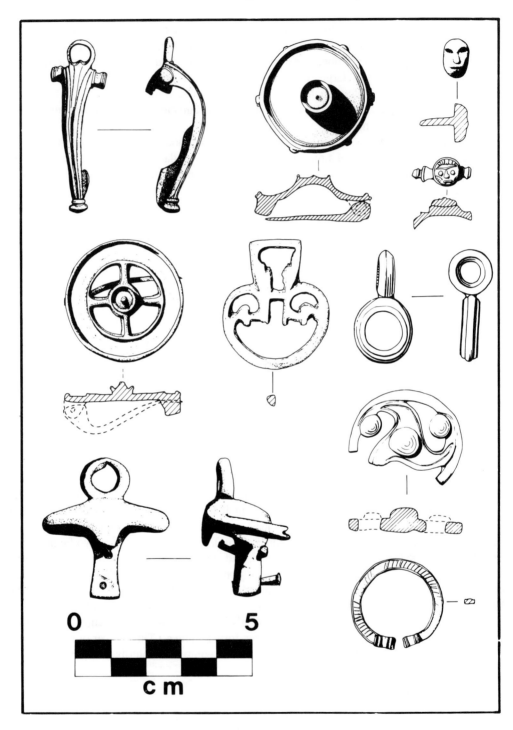

Figure 3.3   A selection of bronzework from Poole's Cavern, Derbyshire.

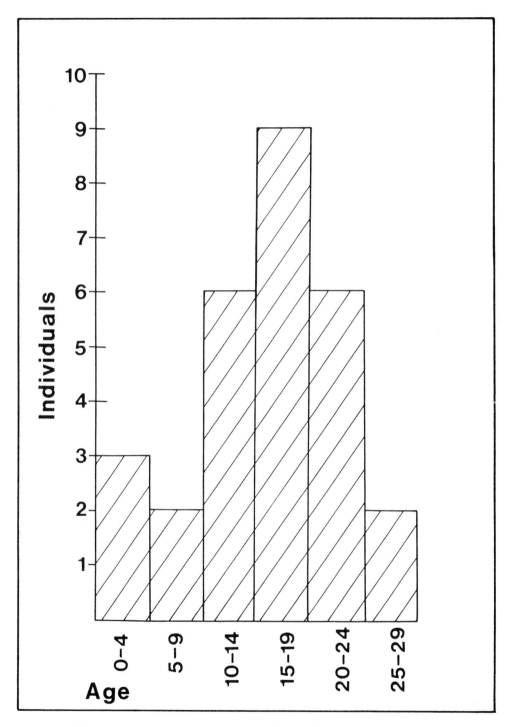

Figure 3.2   Histogram of estimated ages of burials in Wookey Hole 4th Chamber cemetery.

Workshop Usage

We define as workshop usage cave occupation which involves craft activity producing artifacts or materials for trade or exchange in the 'marketplace', whether that means local barter or cash sale at an established marketing centre. As noted above, and anticipated in chapter two, caves which appear to have been used as workshops also produce evidence of domestic occupation. There are craft activities which may be undertaken for purely domestic consumption, and some of these may overlap in the Romano-British economy with crafts producing for the marketplace. Such crafts may include leather-working, wool spinning and weaving, bone-working and both bronze- and iron-smithing. In identifying workshop usage we have therefore taken into consideration not only the criteria discussed in chapter 2 (supra p.16) but also the apparent volume of production and the clientele at which it is seemingly aimed. On this basis we identify six caves as workshops, although two more (N1 Attermire and S10 Long Hole) are suspected as possibly fulfilling this function too.

The evidence for Poole's Cavern, Thirst House, Wookey and Minchin Hole has been discussed in some detail in papers elsewhere (Branigan and Bayley 1989; Branigan and Dearne, 1991a, forthcoming b, Branigan, Dearne and Rutter, forthcoming) and need not be discussed at length here. Poole's Cavern and Thirst House, only five kilometres apart, produced very similar assemblages of bronzework and both appear to have been manufacturing good quality bronze jewellery in some quantity (Figure 3.3). The assemblage from the Victoria and Albert caves, even in its incompletely recorded state, is similar (and larger) but without detailed study is unlikely to reveal the evidence of manufacture that came from Poole's Cavern. An unfinished penannular brooch and some tools might be indicative of what might emerge from a detailed study of the full assemblage. The sheer quantity of quality bronzework, however, points clearly to production for the marketplace.

Metalworking, with bronze, lead and iron, also took place at Wookey Hole but here there is insufficient evidence to confirm production for other than domestic use. The collection of iron tools suitable for carpentry is interesting but has the same limitations. Equally intriguing but difficult to assess are the thirty spindle whorls and thirteen unfinished examples ascribed to the Romano-British occupation of the cave. Wool production and spinning comes as no surprise on the edge of Mendip and the quantity of whorls is suggestive of production on a considerable scale but this is difficult to confirm. The other craft activity likely to be producing for a market beyond the cave is bone-working. Almost 60 bone pins and needles are identified as probably Romano-British, and there may well be other products amongst the bone collection from the cave, which includes Iron Age material of course. The inclusion of Wookey in our list of workshops is based on the impression of considerable activity in five or six crafts, which in at least two cases – wool production and bone-working – seems likely to have been on a scale sufficient to produce a marketable surplus.

The designation of Minchin Hole as a workshop is made on a somewhat similar basis. There is limited evidence of bronze- and iron-smithing, of carpentry, leather-working and wool production; none of this seems likely to have have been primarily for market consumption. Again it is the bone working that attracts attention but here it is not the quantity but rather the quality that suggests a commercial incentive. Amongst the twenty-five bone items recovered were eight spoons, six of which are exceptionally fine (Figure 3.4). It is difficult to envisage these delicate spoons having any place in the workaday routine of the cave occupants and we are

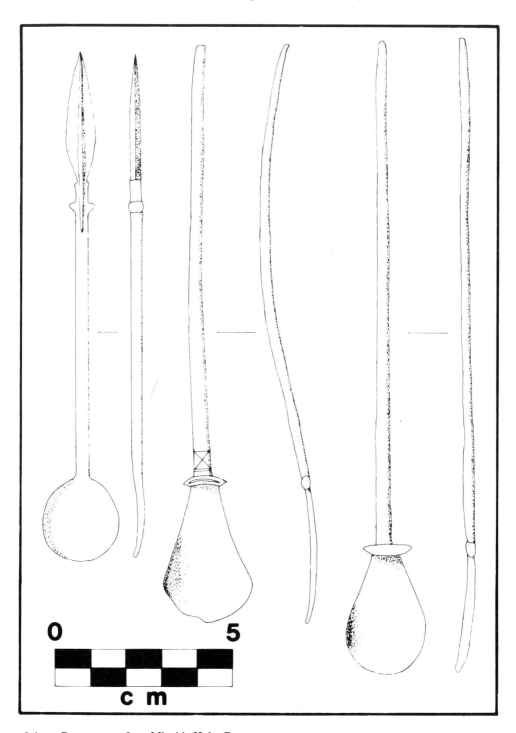

Figure 3.4   Bone spoons from Minchin Hole, Gower.

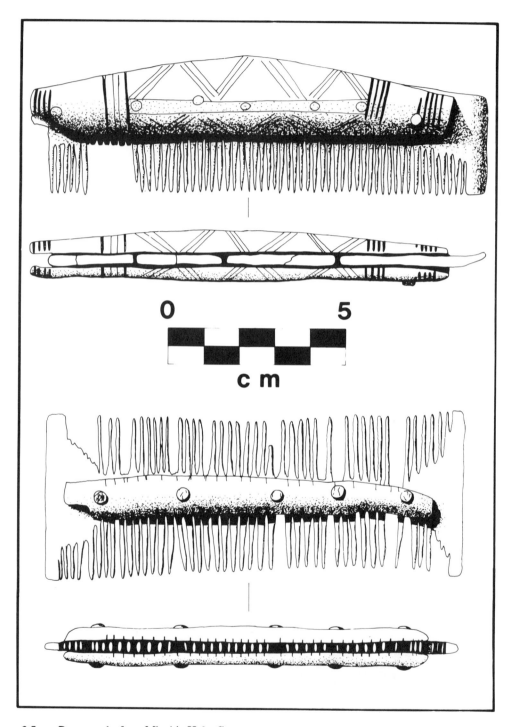

Figure 3.5   Bone combs from Minchin Hole, Gower.

convinced they were being produced, possibly with combs (Figure 3.5), for the Romanised marketplace.

As to the temporal nature of workshop usage we can only repeat the comments made above in discussing domestic usage sites. All the workshop sites appear to have prolonged usage, though we cannot be sure for how long specific craft activities were pursued, but whether seasonal use was involved we cannot ascertain.

Storage Caves

Archaeological identification of caves used for the storage of organic foodstuffs and materials, which is the most likely material to have been stored in caves in the Romano-British period, is particularly difficult. The best hope of identifying such usage would be the recognition of the relevant plant remains or insect fauna associated with the storage of specific crops. Quite apart from the problems of interpreting such plant or insect assemblages in our present state of ignorance of cave taphonomy, to be of any value such assemblages would have to come from sealed, undisturbed Romano-British deposits and there are very few of those yet identified in caves. We are thrown back then on the criteria which we set out in our discussion of the storage model in chapter two (supra p.17). Given these criteria, the only caves which we feel tempted to identify as storage caves are three in the gorge at Creswell Crags. Church Hole, Pin Hole and Mother Grundy's Parlour (P7, 8, 10) are all accessible and have produced a few personal trinkets and a handful of pottery sherds. There is at least one known open site overlooking the gorge for which they could have provided useful storage facilities.

Occasional Shelter

We envisage that the use of caves for occasional shelter will encompass a range of usage from the irregular visits created by immediate and passing circumstances (storms, blizzards etc) to a more pre-determined use such as seasonal sleeping sites by shepherds who nevertheless have their habitation site, even at this season of the year, elsewhere. Caves might also be occupied for occasional shelter where they are adjacent to a trackway or road. For any of these usages to be likely to leave artifactual debris, however, the caves must probably have been well known as shelter places, so that usage, though spasmodic took place over a long period of time. We discussed in chapter 2 the sort of evidence that one might expect such usage to produce – the odd dropped trinket or coin, simple tools, a small quantity of pottery and evidence of meals and fires. We identify thirty-one caves which were probably so used during the Romano-British era, and which were not utilised in other ways. Of all the usages proposed, however, it must be said that occasional shelter is the easiest to suggest but the hardest to convincingly demonstrate. It is also the identification most likely to be overturned by new excavations, since to an extent its identification rests on an absence, or at least scarcity, of evidence.

A brief look at some of the caves we identify as occasional shelters may serve to underline these difficulties, whilst also giving an impression of the sort of assemblage of evidence that we have found suggestive of this usage. Amongst the caves of south Wales, Lesser Garth Cave (W6) provides an interesting example. The material included only pottery, stone implements, and probably faunal material. A minimum number of eighteen vessels can be identified in the pottery, mostly cooking pots, and these are spread over a period from the late first century to the third/fourth century; the majority are probably of third/fourth century date. The stone implements included five rubbers, a pounder and two whetstones, perhaps associated with the preparation and cooking of food. The faunal remains, including ox, pig, and sheep/goat, probably included Romano-British food debris though they are not from a sealed context. Hearths near the cave entrance were associated with Romano-British pottery. Hussey (1966), who excavated the cave, noted the proximity of iron-ore deposits and suggested that Romano-British usage might be associated with mining activity. If the deposits were utilised in the Roman period, then use of the cave as an occasional shelter is certainly a possibility.

In the Mendips, Badger Hole (S4) near Wookey presents a typical assemblage. The pottery group here too represents a minimum of about seventeen vessels, but is rather more varied than that at Lesser Garth. Whilst bowls and jars in cooking pot wares predominate, followed by storage jars, there are single examples of a mortarium and a flagon, and remains of three samian vessels. As with Lesser Garth, the pottery ranges from the later first to the third century. Other finds are few but varied – a bronze fibula, a third century coin, a hone and possibly a handful of iron artifacts, though the date of these is dubious. The least convincing aspect of this cave as an occasional shelter is its location, close to Wookey Hole, and with an open site situated above the rock face in which the cave is situated. But the chronological spread of the small quantity of pottery and the handful of personal belongings, together with no evidence of burials, still suggest occasional shelter as the most likely usage.

A final example, from the Peak District, is Beeston Tor Cave (P3). A small collection of pot sherds represents seven vessels, including two samian bowls and four or five jars. A melon bead, bone awl and antler knife handle are the only other certain Romano-British finds, although a lost fibula and coins could be Roman. Both animal and human bones are from mixed deposits in a cave which may have been used in the Bronze Age, Iron Age and Saxon periods too. In any event, the cave is not well located as a hideaway, has produced no evidence of ritual usage, and on the present evidence is unconvincing as a domestic occupation site. Use as an occasional shelter seems more likely than funerary usage on present evidence.

Hideaways

In our discussion of hideaway usage in chapter two we essentially identified two main variations. In one the cave is used as a temporary occupation site by fugitives; in the other a cave is used as a place in which to hide valuables. In both cases caves which are difficult of access and have disguised entrances are most likely to be used, but in the case of hideaways for fugitives such entrances are almost a prerequisite.

Somewhat to our surprise we eventually identified twenty four caves as fulfilling a hideaway function. Five, perhaps six, of these caves produced coin hoards and two of these need further discussion. The remaining caves produced assemblages comprising small quantities of pottery and personal belongings, the latter normally present in greater quantity than in caves we have identified as occasional shelters. Bones of domesticates were found in many of the caves but as usual they can rarely be firmly associated with Romano-British occupation. Classic examples of the group may include Sun Hole (S13) and Soldiers Hole (S12) in Cheddar Gorge, both perched high in the wall of the gorge, and very difficult of access. It is impossible to be certain how well disguised their entrances were in the Roman period but they may well have been at least as difficult to spot as they are today. Sun Hole produced remains of eight pottery vessels, three or four coins, and a shale bracelet, whilst Soldiers Hole yielded but a single jar, coin, and bronze pin, plus two spindle whorls, three bone counters and a needle. It may be remembered that Soldier's Hole is so-called because tradition associates it with a fugitive from Monmouth's rebel army.

Old Woman's House (P20) in Taddington Dale, Derbyshire, provides a good example of a hideaway cave which is not remote or inaccessible but has a very small and well disguised entrance. Equally it is a small, and almost totally dark cave and unlikely to be used for any domestic occupation or even occasional shelter. Yet there is nothing from it to suggest funerary or ritual usage, and the quantity of material is sufficient to suggest that it was at some point occupied for a time, presumably therefore as a hideaway. Three or four pottery vessels are represented, along with a few iron and bone tools, three bronze brooches and several coins, three spindle-whorls and two whetstones. At least some of the faunal sample was presumably of Roman date.

Perhaps the best excavated of the classic 'hideaways' is Ossum's Eyrie Cave (P22) in the Manifold Valley (Bramwell 1958). The cave is perched 30m up a cliff face and fronted by a narrow ledge; the excavators reached it with a 10m rope ladder lowered from the cliff top. The entrance is only 2m wide and little more than 1m high, and the area that can be occupied measures little more than about 5m^2. Excavation found that the debris from Roman usage was in fact concentrated by the mouth. A 'mass of charcoal' was presumably traces of a hearth on which food had been prepared; bones of sheep and pig were found in this level. Personal belongings were at a minimum – a bone pin and bronze brooch, an iron knife, stone ornament (?), and a single potsherd (was the rest of the vessel tossed over the ledge when it was broken ?).

Of the caves producing coin hoards four are in one way or another unsatisfactory, indeed in one case we do not know the name or exact location of the cave, simply that it was in Dry Dale in the Peak (P19). A fourth century hoard of at least 9 coins was recovered but all are now lost. The other example from the Peak District, Reynard's Cave (P26) is said by Wilson (1926) to have produced a hoard of Roman coins but no details are known. Apart from this it yielded a handful of bronze, iron, lead and bone artifacts and a somewhat larger pottery assemblage, as well as a faunal assemblage of uncertain, probably mixed, date. It is possible that the hoard and the other material represent two different periods of usage, and therefore perhaps two different types of usage but in the absence of any information about the hoard it is impossible to say. Uphill Quarry Cave 2 (S24) is at the base of a south facing cliff near Brean Down (Somerset) and produced what is almost certainly a hoard of late fourth century coins, numbering in excess of 129 and perhaps originally buried in a pottery vessel. No finds survive from this cave. The fourth cave hoard came from Pride Evans' Hole in Cheddar Gorge. It is poorly documented (Dobson 1931, 156, 236), and again does not survive. It allegedly consisted of 47 coins from Gallienus to Tetricus II, but the supposed find circumstances are difficult to credit in view both of Pride Evans' domestic occupation of the cave and of Balch's exploration of it.

The remaining two caves in this category are rather different. The most clearly documented and studied is White Woman's Hole, Mendip (S25). This small and discrete cave with an entrance less than a metre square produced sherds of four pottery vessels, the head of an iron pin, and more than four hundred pieces of bronze counterfeiting debris which included coins, counterfiet coins, flans, small bronze rods and pieces of scrap. These included a group or hoard of 76 counterfeit late third century Antoniniani, and a group of 45 Constantinian counterfeits.

Boon (Barrett and Boon 1972, 79) believes that the whole deposit probably dates to the middle of the fourth century and the earlier counterfeit material was here as scrap to be used for a new counterfeit issue. In addition there were eight coins not apparently directly connected with the counterfeiting activity, the latest of which (Arcadius) must represent casual usage. In view of the absence of any crucible fragments, clay moulds and dies production of coins at the cave cannot be envisaged; rather this must represent the hiding place of incriminating material which was brought from a counterfeiting site elsewhere.

One other known counterfeiting site in this area is at Whitchurch, where an open site yielded coin moulds for Gallic Empire antoniniani and was probably in production around AD 275 (Boon and Rahtz 1966). There is a possibility that to these might be added a third site, Rowberrow Cavern (S19). This cave in the Mendips has a large entrance and may well have been easier to find in the Roman period than it is today. The assemblage from it, however, is most unusual and not easily equated with domestic, ritual or funerary usage. About twenty vessels may have been represented in the pottery assemblage but apart from a piece of lead strip and faunal remains of uncertain date the rest of the finds are coins, fragmentary coins and bronze waste. The coins, as recorded, are all of the late third century. The twenty-three recorded pieces include two 'copies', three 'imitations', three half coins and eight fragments. It is the latter items than immediately recall the White Woman's Hole material in which many half and quarter fragments were found, and could here be directly related to the specific method of counterfeiting being used. One would give much to examine the Rowberrow coins but they, and all the other material from the cave, were lost during war-time bombing of the Bristol University Spelaeological Museum. If the Rowberrow finds were part of the stock-in-trade of a counterfeiter then he may have been using the same, somewhat unusual, technique of producing his illegal money, as the counterfeiter who hid his materials in White Woman's Hole.

We have not discussed the temporal nature of the hideaway usage since we believe that almost by definition it will have been episodic. There is nothing from the assemblages of the twenty-two caves included in this group to suggest otherwise.

Ritual Usage

The palaeolithic cave paintings of southern Europe, the importance of certain caves in Minoan religion, and the on-going use of caves in some parts of the world for religious purposes might encourage us to search for evidence of ritual usage in the Romano-British period. Bramwell et al (1983) suggested that Poole's Cavern may have been used as a shrine, but the arguments on which this proposal was made were refuted by Branigan and Bayley (1989, 48–9) in their study of the metalwork from the site. At no cave with Romano-British usage have we found evidence of discrete deposits of possible offerings or votive material, or of natural rock or stalagmite formations being the focus of activity. Only one site has produced an artifact with clear religious associations and that is Culver Hole (W3). Here was found a small bronze figurine of a naked female; she cannot be identified with any specific goddess in the Roman or Romano-Celtic pantheon. The figurine was found in a small boulder-surrounded pool to the left of the entrance, from which pool also came eleven coins (possibly part of a small fourth century hoard), a boars tusk and a 16cm long iron rod. Other finds included three (or four) bronze brooches, a bracelet, five other coins, a spindle whorl and a glass bead.

Three of the coins and at least two of the brooches fall within the second century and seem likely to represent a separate episode to the fourth century 'hoard'. The figurine is presumed to belong chronologically with the fourth century coins with which it was found. On the present, somewhat confused, evidence available we might identify a fourth century episode of ritual usage, preceded by a second century use the character of which is uncertain. The cave itself is only 6m above the sea and difficult of access except at low tide; high tides and stormy seas enter the cave and this makes it unsuitable for occupation.

Burial

Due to the disturbed nature of most cave deposits it is often difficult to be certain as to whether human skeletal material is to be associated with Romano-British usage or whether it belongs to either pre- or post-Roman activity. Equally, even in caves with exclusively Romano-British artifact assemblages, where the material brackets a long period of time then it is difficult to ascertain with which material any skeletal remains belong. We have sought to identify the material in the overall assemblage which was most likely to have been part of the funerary deposits, and use that as a guide to the date of the burial usage, but such deductions must obviously be tentative.

We have identified eighteen caves which we think were used for burial at some time in the Roman period. There are other caves which produce Romano-British material and have also yielded human skeletal remains but for various reasons we believe there is probably no connection between the human remains and the Romano-British use of the cave. Of the eighteen caves that we do place in this group, at least six and probably eight were also used in the Roman era for other functions. In most instances there are clear indications of either spatial or chronological separation of burials from other activities.

Although the amount of information about the skeletal remains varies from full specialist reports to little more than a passing mention, it appears that the cave burial deposits can be placed in three categories according to the number of burials attested. Four caves appear to have upward of 20 burials, five have between 6 and 12, and six have between 1 and 4. If we were able to sharpen the chronological focus on these burials then we might be able to tentatively reconstruct the size of the contributing population but few caves offer any hope of such definition. We suggest, however, that the caves with 1 to 4 burials are most likely to represent very short-lived usage by a single family, those with 6 to 10 burials family usage over a generation or two and the larger groups usage by two or three families over a similar period of time. These suggestions are made on the basis of a nuclear family probably contributing twenty bodies per century to a burial place (Bintliff in Blackman and Branigan 1977, 84).

Examples of a short-lived burial episode are Fairy Hole (N6), Thirst House (P28), Charterhouse Warren Farm Swallett (S7), and Ogof-yr-Ychen (W17). In Fairy Hole there were two individuals, remains of two pottery vessels and an iron pin; the cave is low and narrow and unsuitable for most purposes. At Thirst House the four burials were all found on the steep slope immediately below the cave, and might therefore be excluded from consideration, but they clearly relate to the usage of the cave.

Charterhouse Warren Farm Swallett is a short, low side-passage off a vertical shaft of little use except for burials or a hideaway for valuables. Amongst prehistoric material and skeletal remains there was one burial of a male aged c.30 years, associated with two pottery vessels, hobnails, a bronze ring and a shale armlet. Ogof-yr-Ychen has a low ceiling and six small chambers; a child burial was found associated with Romano-British pottery in chamber 4.

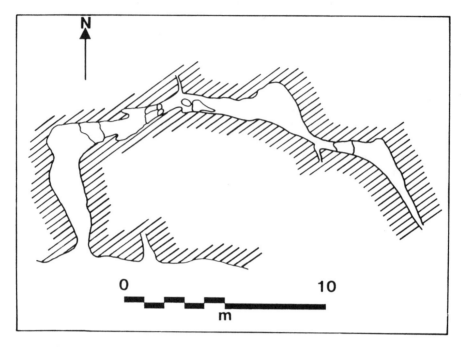

Figure 3.6   Plan of Frank i'th' Rocks cave, Derbyshire.

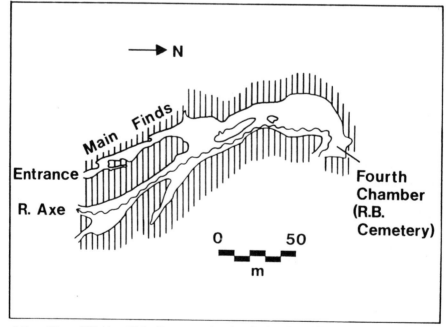

Figure 3.7   Plan of Wookey Hole, Somerset, showing the location of Romano-British material.

The second category of caves can be represented by Frank i'th' Rocks (P17) and Maeshafn (W10). Frank i'th' Rocks is a long, very narrow cave which turns through 90° about a quarter of the way along it from the entrance (Figure 3.6). The assemblage includes ten fourth century coins, which do not easily associate with remains of two samian vessels, one or two second century coarseware pots and an early second century fibula. It may be that the cave saw two separate episodes of usage. One of these was presumably for burials since remains of about ten individuals, mostly children, were found. A handful of stone and iron tools might relate to use as an occasional shelter, but it is difficult to decide which usage was more likely to be associated with the second century pottery and brooch, although orthodox opinion would probably place the skeletal remains in the fourth century. Maeshafen Cave is another which is essentially a narrow fissure with a twisting passage. Remains of six individuals, including children, were recovered. The only artifact material was three bronze brooches and a ring, the former suggesting a date in the late first to later second century AD.

The caves which suggest prolonged usage by perhaps more than one family group include Dog Holes, Haverbrack (N4), Wookey Hole (S26) and Ogof-yr-Esgyrn (W16). Dog Holes is entered by a vertical shaft over 6m deep. The remains of more than 23 individuals were discovered here, aged from about 6 to 50+ years. Finds included six bronze armlets and two rings, an iron brooch and some studs, jet beads and two whetstones. Three dozen glass beads of probably Saxon date mean that we cannot be sure that all the skeletal remains are Roman.

At Wookey Hole the fourth century burials were made in the fourth chamber, further into the cave than the domestic occupation areas, and they are dated by the material found with them (Figure 3.7). This group is important, therefore, as it provides one of the very few clear snapshots of an assemblage from a cave cemetery. There were about a dozen pottery vessels recovered, fourteen coins, five finger rings, a bracelet, brooch, shale armlet, hob nails and glass and jet beads. These were associated with the remains of more than twenty-eight individuals, aged from 6 months to 35 years. It is likely, however, that some of the 19+ individuals represented by human skeletal material recovered from the river which flows through the cave were washed off the bank in the fourth chamber.

Like Wookey, Ogof-yr-Esgyrn was used for both domestic occupation and burials but here the separation of the two functions was essentially chronological rather than spatial, although the burials were found in a discrete group against the wall of the chamber. The amount of material found in situ with the skeletal remains was small – a dolphin brooch, a sestertius of Trajan, two iron finger-rings, an iron pin, a bone ring and bone pin – but other early material is likely to have come from the original grave depositions. This includes five further Flavian – Hadrianic coins, five fibulae, and fragments of half a dozen pottery vessels.

There are common features which link most of these cave burials together. The first is the dominance of inhumations; we have no certain evidence of cremations in caves at all. The second is the nature of the associated material, in which personal jewellery is usually a significant element. At Wookey finger rings and bangles were found still in-situ on finger-bones and forearms. Thirdly, in the case of the smaller grave groups, the caves are notably small, narrow and of little use for other purposes except temporary shelter or hideaways.

We might also note that at least eight of the burial caves also have Iron Age usage, which in four or five cases is thought or known to include burials. It may be that we see here a continuity of tradition. The tradition of using caves for burials was already long-established in north Britain in the Iron Age. Gilks (1989) has documented fifty Late Neolithic burial caves and rock shelters in the region and a further seven Early Bronze Age examples, and comments on their occurrence elsewhere including south-west England and Wales. Whether or not continuity of tradition also points to chronological continuity of usage is a topic which is best addressed in the following chapter.

Conclusions

Our attempts to identify the functions which caves served in Roman Britain have led to a list which suggests that the commonest usage was as places of occasional shelter. More than one in three of the caves studied seem to have been used in that way. A more surprising conclusion perhaps is that of the other uses to which caves were put, hideaways and domestic occupation are as frequent as burials, and far more so than ritual usage. Given the widespread Romano-British use of stone-founded buildings, particularly in the limestone areas, domestic occupation of caves seems an anachronism. Yet our survey of recent and modern cave usage shows that caves continue to offer attractions for occupation. The frequency of 'hideaways' in the Roman period might at first suggest a higher level of unrest or lawlessness that we generally suppose in the province of Britain. But the half dozen examples of caves used to hide hoards cannot be used to support that contention, anymore than can the much greater number of hoards found at non-cave sites. The counterfeiting activities at White Woman's Hole and perhaps Rowberrow certainly have a clandestine aspect, but the circumstances which induced the hideaway usage of the remaining fourteen or fifteen caves are probably unrecoverable to the archaeologist. They should not be assumed to be associated with either criminal activities or military prosecution without further evidence. As for burial usage we have already noted that this may, at least in some regions, represent a continuity of tradition. Similarly, the scarcity of ritual usage (other than for funerary purposes) might be said to continue the lack of interest in caves as places of ritual displayed in the Iron Age. Despite evidence of Iron Age usage from many caves, there is no good evidence that this usage was ritual. Ross' (1974, 142) suggestion of a ritual significance for the skulls recovered from the stream in Wookey Hole is not accepted here, since we believe these skulls were probably washed from the cemetery area in chamber 4. Finally we suggest that the small number of caves in which evidence for workshop activity has been found may be an under-representation of workshop usage. Few caves have been excavated in recent years and it is possible that some iron tools, for example, were not recognised as such by their earlier excavators and that some residues from craft activities were not recognised or recorded. Many of the documented examples of recent cave usage reveal some craft activity associated with domestic occupation of caves and there are certainly hints of it in the surviving assemblages from caves other than those we have suggested were used as workshops. In most instances, however, such activities may well have been for immediate domestic consumption and should therefore be seen as no more than an aspect of domestic occupation.

It is of course evident that some caves fulfilled more than one function. Usually this means that at different times within the Roman era a cave may have served as a home and as a burial place. Occasionally a cave served two functions at the same time, like Wookey with its occupation and its burial areas and Poole's Cavern and the other caves used as workshops which also provided domestic occupation. Almost certainly many caves for which only one function can presently be identified in the archaeological record may have served others which cannot now be detected. The most obvious example will be where a cave used for domestic occupation was used, perhaps only a decade or two later for occasional shelter, but there are other situations which can easily be envisaged which would be equally unidentifiable. These complications in the record of usage also complicate our understanding of the chronology of cave use in Roman Britain as we shall see in the next chapter.

4.   Romano-British Cave Usage – Chronological and Spatial Analysis

As with the functional analysis of cave usage, discussion of the chronology of cave utilisation is limited by the nature and quality of the evidence. The incomplete records, the lost material, and the paucity of dateable artifacts are problems which have to be faced with the majority of the sites in our catalogue. In assessing such evidence as is available we have attempted to grade it Poor (P), Fair (F) or Good (G), although there is inevitably some subjectivity in our choice of gradings. There are many variables in the cultural assemblages which make it difficult to establish any strict criteria for grading. Some pottery is more closely dateable than some bronze jewellery, but the opposite is also true. Coins are normally more closely dateable than pottery or jewellery, but the surviving records on some coins often provide only a broad indication of date. Coins and bronze jewellery are also likely to stay in circulation for longer than pottery, but it can be very difficult to assess how long the circulation period has been. What weighting does one give to the chronological evidence of two coins in comparison to that of twenty pot sherds or two fibulae? There is, of course, no simple answer to such a question – only more questions: which coins, sherds, and fibulae, and what is their condition?

As a general rule, a G grading indicates the evidence of several coins, with the supporting evidence of reasonably closely dated pottery (to within a century bracket) and bronze or ironwork. An F graded assemblage will normally include some coin and bronzework evidence together with distinctive and dateable pot-sherds. A site graded P has usually produced only the odd coin or dateable bronze and a small collection of broadly dateable pottery. Sites graded P are not really very useful – their evidence is simply too weak to be relied on. In our discussion, and in table 3 we only include assemblages which have been rated as at least P/F borderline. Even then, we can propose dating brackets for less than half of our corpus of sites. If we exclude the P/F borderline group we have only twenty-three on which to focus our attention, whilst only eleven rate a borderline F/G or better, and a meagre seven caves are graded as G.

There are further constraints within these severe limitations. In the case of caves we have to be especially aware of the possibility of episodic or recurrent usage as opposed to continuous use – yet our chronological evidence often lacks the sharp definition which will allow us to identify episodic use. Similarly, the disturbed nature of almost all cave deposits means that it is usually impossible to gain any insights from the stratigraphy as to the length of time over which an assemblage broadly dateable to, say, the second century actually accumulated.

Nevertheless, the chronological distribution of Romano-British cave usage is obviously an important aspect of this phenomenon and we must use the evidence as best we can. Fortunately, the spatial distribution of cave usage is more easily considered and it is therefore perhaps best if we first consider spatial patterning.

The Geographical Distribution of Utilised Caves

The distribution of utilised caves in England and Wales broadly reflects the occurrence of caves and therefore the geology of the country. Cave formation in Britain is essentially a phenomenon of Limestone areas and especially of Limestones with massive bedding and jointing, although there are a number of factors including glaciation history, localised hydrology, faulting and the presence or absence of impervious beds, which affect the specific forms and locations of caves.

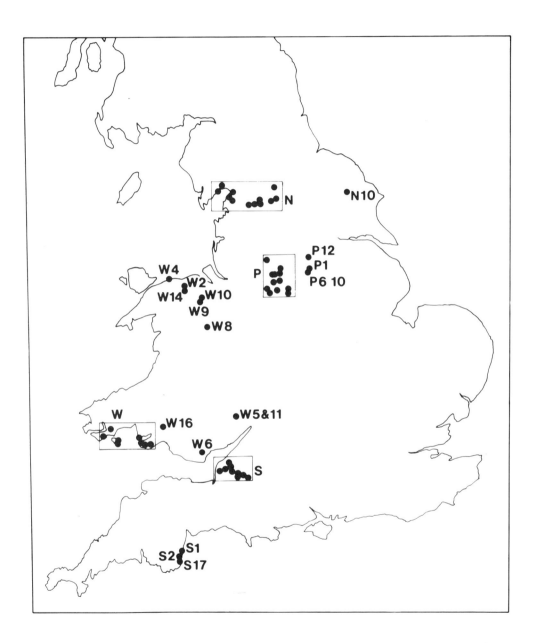

Figure 4.1   Map of England and Wales showing the location of caves with Romano-British material. For details of areas S,W,P and N see pp.121-124.

In many areas of cave occurrence, the forms which the caves take are unsuitable for human utilisation, being of swallet or pot hole form, or still the sites of active water flows.

All of the main areas of significant cave occurrence in Britain appear to have seen Romano-British activity (Figure 4.1). Thus there are particularly significant numbers of utilised caves in N.W. Yorkshire, the Peak District, Gower and the Pembrokeshire coast, the Mendips and in the scattered limestone outcrops of N. Wales. Smaller groups of utilised caves also appear in several of the less significant areas of cave occurrence including one of the six small groups of caves in the Devonian Limestone of S. Devon (the Torquay/Brixham group including Kent's Cavern, Ash Hole and Anstey's Cave), the Creswell Crags group in the Permian Limestones east of the Pennines, the south Cumbrian caves (Kirkhead cavern etc.), the Carboniferous Limestone of Symond's Yat (Merlin's and King Arthur's Caves), and two of the seven main groups of caves in northern and eastern south Wales (the Tawe Valley group: Ogof-yr-Esgyrn; the S.E. Wales caves: Lesser Garth). Only the relatively unimportant King Alfrid's Cave is outside the main distribution of caves in Britain and occurs in a small Limestone outcrop near the Vale of Pickering.

Whilst there are many caves within the main pattern of cave occurrence that did not see Romano-British activity, many were in any case unsuitable for usage. Thus the great number of caves known north of the N. Craven fault in Yorkshire are mainly without sizeable, dry entrances and only the groups at Giggleswick and Attermire/King's Scars, as well as a few outliers such as the 'shaft' cave of Dowkerbottom, were in fact attractive or accessible. Cave usage in pre-Roman times, and particularly in the Late Neolithic/Early Bronze Age appears to have been more intensive. Thus Gilks (1989) maps fifty seven caves utilised at this period in northern England alone, compared to fifty one identified as used in the Romano-British period in this study and the disparity is in fact greater than these figures suggest, since all the caves mapped by Gilks are burial sites, while many of the Romano-British sites probably only saw casual sheltering activity. Indeed, the greater utilisation of caves in the Neolithic and Bronze Ages is at least partly explained by the fact that the usage was primarily for burial and so caves unsuitable for many functions suggested for Romano-British activity were also utilised. Relatively few Romano-British caves had not seen usage in previous periods because they were often relatively large but many caves used in earlier periods were not re-used in Romano-British times.

Certainly there does not seem to be any connection between the distribution of population or the bias of 'Romanisation' within Britain and the usage of caves. Given the basic distribution of the occurrence of caves, utilisation was just as intensive in southern as northern England, and the absence of cave utilisation in south and east England, and indeed mid-Wales, was related not to social or cultural factors, but instead simply reflects the non-occurrence of caves in these areas.

There are, however, some regional variations in cave usage which do call for brief comment. The table below (Table 4.1) summarises the regional distribution of cave use by function; some caves are included twice if we are sure that they filled two different functions.

The use of caves for shelter needs little comment since it is the function one might expect to be most universal and to show least regional variation; it is also that which needs least explanation. Each region, however, seems to have a relative preponderance of one other form of cave usage. In Wales it is burial usage, represented in one in three caves. We tentatively suggest that this may reflect the surviving strength of prehistoric traditions in Wales. In the north of

England domestic occupation is the most frequent usage, almost half the cave usage being in that category.

This may be to some extent a reflection of the prevalence of large caves suitable for habitation in a rather bleak and exposed area around Settle. Somewhat surprisingly, both Mendip and the Peak reveal a considerable use of hideaways; in the Peak a third of cave usage is in this category, whilst in Mendip it is almost as prevalent. We are at a loss to explain this phenomenon unless the common presence of lead and silver mines may be a factor. No doubt there was considerable clandestine activity around such centres, and in Mendip there is even a little evidence for it (Elkington 1976, 192–3). Whether this may have involved the use of cave hideaways is much less certain, and certainly no more than speculation on present evidence.

	Peak Dist.	North England	South-West	Wales
BURIALS	4	3	5	6
HIDEAWAYS	11	2	9	2
SHELTER	11	4	9	7
DOMESTIC	5	8	4	3
STORAGE	3	-	-	-
RITUAL	-	-	-	1
TOTALS	34	17	27	19

Table 4.1   Regional frequency of cave usage by function.

General Aspects of Chronological Distribution

The usage of caves in the Romano-British period does not appear to be concentrated in any one century but to be spread throughout the period.

First century usage is well attested at Victoria and Albert caves (N18), Dowkerbottom (N5), and Ogof-yr-Esgyrn (W16) among others. Many of the forty caves in our Table 4.2 produce evidence of second century use, and at least a dozen can demonstrate third century occupation. The evidence of the latter group is concentrated in the second half of the third century but early third century occupation is notoriously difficult to document unless a site is unusually well endowed with coins. There are sufficient caves which have evidence for late second and late third century use, however, to think that cave usage continued through the first half of the third century unabated. Fourth century cave occupation is attested in more than a dozen cases, often with substantial groups of both coinage and pottery. Wookey Hole (S26), Minchin Hole (W12), and Frank i'th' Rocks (P17) are good examples of this group.

Against this general picture of usage throughout the Roman period must be set the overwhelming evidence that few individual caves were utilised, even episodically, from the first century to the end of the fourth. The caves which appear to have most persistent usage, however sporadic, are Attermire (N1), Dowkerbottom (N5) and Victoria and Albert caves (N18) in the Settle area, Merlin's Cave, Herefordshire (W11), Wookey Hole (S26) and perhaps Long Hole (S10), in the Mendips. If any caves were used more or less continuously throughout the Roman occupation then the most likely candidates are those in the Settle area. Even if the full assemblages from these caves became available for study, however, it is unlikely that more or less continuous usage could be confirmed given the nature of their exploration.

As we noted at the end of the preceding chapter, some caves which exhibit use in both the earlier and later Roman period saw a change in usage. This is most clearly documented where one period of usage was for burial, such as is the case at Ogof-yr-Esgyrn (W16), Frank i'th' Rocks (P17) and Wookey Hole (S26). One suspects that many caves with a substantial assemblage belonging to one period and a minor one belonging to another may have seen a change of usage but it would be difficult to identify this in view of the difficulty of dating some of the key evidence for usage, such as tools, craft residues and faunal samples.

The remaining problem of continuity to be addressed is the extent of continuity of cave usage at either end of the Roman occupation. In some areas, such as Mendip, there is considerable evidence for Iron Age use of caves (Fowler 1970, 21) and it might be expected that such use would continue after the Roman conquest. One example of such continuity might be the burials in Backwell Cave (S3)which appear to bridge the late Iron Age and early Roman period. On present evidence, however, this would seem to be an exception. The evidence from Read's Cavern shows no Romano-British usage, whilst at Rowberrow (S19) and Sun Hole (S13)the Romano-British activity was clearly of the later third century. Most significantly, the substantial Iron Age and Romano-British usages of Wookey Hole (S26)appear to be clearly separated in time when the evidence is carefully sifted, with the first episode of Romano-British usage coming in the first half of the second century (Branigan and Dearne forthcoming a).

When we turn attention northwards problems arise because of the uncertain dating of much of the later Iron Age material, some of which may have continued in use after the Roman conquest, at least into the second half of the first century AD. Nevertheless there still seems to be a recognisable gap in usage at sites like Elderbush Cave (P14) and Thors Cave (P29). The latter may have seen significant Iron Age use, but apart from uncertainty about the date of the latest Iron Age material, all the Romano-British artifacts to which a date can be assigned seem to be no earlier than the second century but for a single fibula. In the Settle caves such as Attermire (N1) and Dowkerbottom (N5)the first Romano-British usage seems to be earlier, in the second half of the first century, and here there must be the possibility of continuity from Iron Age usage. The principal problem lies with the difficulty of assigning close dates to the latest Iron Age material rather than with the opening dates for Romano-British occupation. If continuity of use from Iron Age to Roman occurred in any of the British cave groups, it is most likely in North Yorkshire.

Continuity from the Roman to the Saxon or the Post-Roman era is even more difficult to identify. Almost all the caves which saw Romano-British use lie outside the areas of early Anglo-Saxon settlement. Such Saxon material as occurs therefore tends to be relatively late. Of the thirteen caves used in the Roman period which have also produced Saxon material, only Minchin Hole can be convincingly argued to have been occupied in the immediately post-Roman period. The bone combs from this site and perhaps some of the calcite-gritted ware suggest early fifth century occupation. Even here, true Anglo-Saxon material – in this case three coins – is of much later date. Such Saxon usage as there was seems commonest in the Peak District and south Wales, but it never seems to have been an important part of the Saxon settlement pattern.

In general terms the probability of Romano-British cave usage being part of a continuum with either pre-Roman or post-Roman settlement patterns might be most simply assessed by comparing the frequency of caves with Iron Age and Roman assemblages with that of caves with Roman and Saxon assemblages. There are forty-nine of the former and only thirteen of the latter. We believe this may broadly represent the relative strength of continuity of tradition in cave usage between these three periods.

Regional Perspectives

So far we have discussed the chronology of cave usage in general terms, but it is necessary to give some consideration to the possibility of regional variations in the chronology of cave occupation. Although the four main areas of cave utilisation share a common geology and similar patterns of land-use, their experience of the Roman occupation and its consequences was somewhat varied.

In Mendip the Roman military presence was short-lived except perhaps for small detachments of troops needed at Charterhouse and to oversee other imperial interests in the area (Elkington 1976, 184–86, and Branigan 1976, 45). Later this area developed into one of the greatest concentrations of villa estates in the province (Branigan 1976, 21–31)although Mendip itself saw few of them. In south Wales the Roman military occupation came later, in the early Flavian period and although the number of troops was later reduced in this area civilian development in terms of towns and villas remained low-key west of Caerleon. Roman occupation of the Peak district of Derbyshire came in the later 70's following the establishment of forts around the fringes of the area in the preceding two decades. The subsequent development of a small spa at Buxton was the only notable civilian development in terms of Romanisation, but there is the possibility of a colonisation of the area by peoples perhaps from the east midlands in the early-mid second century (Hodges and Wildgoose 1980). The military presence was greatly reduced by the mid second century, although Brough-on-Noe saw prolonged occupation (Hart 1981, 83–90). As for northern England, the Romans penetrated these areas and garrisoned them in the later 70's. Some forts, including Elslack and Ilkley, were decommissioned when Hadrian's Wall was garrisoned in the 120's, but the detailed effects of the Antonine changes of frontier policy are disputed (c.f. Frere 1987, 142; Hartley and Fitts 1988, 29). In any event a military presence was never far away and civilian urban development was restricted mainly to vici. The caves of the Cumbrian/Lancaster border and of the Settle area were well away from the only significant concentration of villa estates in northern England (Branigan 1980); Kirk Sink villa at Gargrave is the most westerly outlier of the group (Hartley and Fitts, 1988, 74–5).

Against these somewhat varying backgrounds we can set our regional variations in the chronology of cave use. In doing so we should perhaps give least weight to cave usage for occasional shelter, since this seems likely to have been irregular and the least likely use to be affected by other aspects of social and political development. In the Mendips cave usage is concentrated heavily in the late third and fourth centuries, and apart from three occasional shelters the only clear evidence of earlier use is at Wookey Hole (S26) in the second century. South Wales presents an immediate contrast with all five caves for which dating evidence is available showing some usage in the later first or second century. But all five caves also reveal later use, probably with a period of at least a century separating the two phases except perhaps in the case of Nanna's Cave (W13). In the Peak district a third pattern may emerge, for here the majority of caves are used in the second century with a little evidence for use in the later third at two or three caves and only two caves suggesting even occasional shelter usage in the fourth. The northern caves are somewhat different again. They provide the best evidence for later first century occupation, and useage then seems to continue, no doubt with some gaps, until at least the end of the third century but probably into the fourth in most cases.

It is difficult to offer convincing explanations of these perceived regional variations, and it is tempting to avoid doing so by claiming that the number of caves for which reliable dating is available is too small to allow of any confidence in the observed patterns. But that is itself an unconvincing position to adopt. The very fact that there are regional variations through time suggests that the explanation does not lie with general political, military or economic developments, or with specific political or military events which were of province-wide significance. Thus there is no suggestion, for example, that the occupation or use of caves was directly related to the advance of the Roman armies into these different regions, or to the onset of the Gallic empire, or to the inflationary spiral of the third century. If explanations are to be sought they must be found either in the identification of functional variations through time or in the context of regional patterns of development.

There appear to be few functional variations through time, with the exception of burial usage. This seems to be concentrated heavily in the first and second centuries AD, regardless of the region in which it is found. As we noted in the preceding chapter (supra p.37) cave burials may be a continuity of prehistoric tradition, and if that were the case then one would expect to find a predominance of early, as opposed to late, Roman examples of this usage. There is perhaps a suggestion of hideaway usage becoming commoner in the late third and fourth centuries, but the dateable sample of hideaways is small (only eight caves)and the six late Roman examples cover a period of at least a century. Furthermore three of the six were classified as 'hideaways' because they produced only hoards of coins, and we have already commented (supra 37) on the dangers of assuming that such hoards reflect on the level of lawlessness in the province. Two of the remaining hideaways can be explained in chronological terms however since they relate directly to documented economic factors. These are the counterfeiting sites at White Woman's Hole (S25) and Rowberrow (S19), the economic and monetary context of which is discussed by Boon (Barrett and Boon 1972, 75–79).

With these few exceptions – burials and counterfeiting hideaways – it seems more likely that regional variations in the chronology of cave usage can be best understood by placing them within their regional context, and this we attempt to do in the following chapter.

		Grade	50	100	150	200	250	300	350	400

Peak District

Cave	Code	Grade
Beeston Tor Cave	(P3)	F
Elderbush Cave	(P14)	F/P
Fox Hole Cave	(P16)	F
Frank-i-th-Rocks	(P17)	F
Harborough Cave	(P18)	F/P
Drydale Cave	(P19)	F
Old Woman's Cave	(P20)	F/P
Ossum's Crag Cave	(P21)	F
Poole's Cavern	(P23)	G
Thirst House Cave	(P28)	G
Thor's Cave	(P29)	G/F
Thor's Fissure	(P30)	F/P
Wetton Mill R.S.	(P32)	F

S. Yorks/N. Notts

Cave	Code	Grade
Church Hole Cave	(P7)	F/P
Pin Hole Cave	(P8)	F/P
Robin Hood's Cave	(P9)	F/P

Mendips

Cave	Code	Grade
Backwell Cave	(S3)	F/P
Badger Hole	(S4)	F/P
Browne's Hole	(S5)	F
Chelm's Combe R.S.	(S14)	F/P
Long Hole/Slitter	(S10)	F/G
Pride Evans' Hole	(S11)	G
Rowberrow Cavern	(S19)	F/P
Tom Tivy's Hole	(S23)	F/P
Uphill Quarry Caves	(S24)	F
White Woman's Hole	(S25)	F/G
Wookey Hole	(S26)	G
Wookey 4th Chamber	(S26)	G

S. W. Britain

Cave	Code	Grade
Kents Cavern	(S17)	F/P

N. England

Cave	Code	Grade
Attermire Cave	(N1)	F
Dog Holes, Warton	(N3)	P/F
Dowkerbottom Hole	(N5)	F
Sewell's Cave	(N15)	F
Victoria & Albert Caves	(N18)	F

Wales

Cave	Code	Grade
Culver Hole	(W3)	P/F
Minchin Hole	(W12)	G
Nanna's Cave	(W13)	F/P
Ogof-yr-Esgryn	(W16)	G
Paviland Cave	(W18)	F/P

Herefordshire

Cave	Code	Grade
Merlin's Cave	(W11)	F/G

Table 4.2   Suggested chronology of 40 caves. (for description of grades, see p.38)

5.   Romano-British Caves and the Wider World

None of the varying functions served by caves and discussed in chapter four took place in a vacuum, and in various ways and to varying degrees each required a working relationship between open (i.e. non-cave) settlements and the cave usage. Caves used for burials or as shrines, for example, must have had contributing populations, and those who occupied caves as homes and workshops must have maintained some economic intercourse with nearby farms, villages and perhaps towns and forts. In this final chapter we seek to explore some of these relationships both in general and specific terms.

The particular problems we face here are threefold. First we have to establish the occurrence of open sites within a reasonable radius of our cave sites. In some areas, such as Mendip, that is easier than others because the archaeological record is better, but even here we have to assume that the record is by no means complete. It is precisely the small, single farmsteads which might be expected to relate most closely to cave usage for hideaways and occasional shelters that are the most difficult to identify from survey data and have attracted least attention from archaeologists of the Roman period.

The second difficulty is the dating of many of the smaller rural settlements. In the Peak District, for example, survey work over the last fifteen years has added many such sites to the distribution map but we cannot distinguish between those of the Iron Age and Roman periods in many cases. Some, which we ascribe to the Romano-British horizon, could even be pre-Iron Age – in the absence of excavation and cultural material we cannot be sure. Even where we have evidence of Romano-British date, we can often ascribe only the most tentative date within the Roman period and such a date will bracket a period of at least a century. This is our third problem – that even where we have adjacent cave and open sites of '2nd century' date, we cannot be at all confident that they were occupied and used simultaneously. Thus, although we attempt to explore specific cave/open-site relationships, we do so in hope rather than in expectation.

Cave Usage and Regional Settlement Chronology

It is perhaps easiest and most sensible to begin by relating the chronology of cave usage to that of open settlements in each of the main regions of cave usage under examination. Such an exercise should provide some indication as to how far cave usage was part of the mainstream of Romano-British settlement history in a given area.

Until relatively recently, Romano-British rural settlement in the Peak District was almost unknown. Although considerable numbers of Romano-British settlements are now known in the region, principally through the efforts of Butcher (Bestwick and Merills 1983) and Makepeace (1985; c.f. also Hart 1981; Branigan 1991) only limited information is available about most of these sites. Excavated examples are confined to Staden near Buxton (Makepeace 1983, 1987, 1989), Roystone Grange (Hodges and Wildgoose 1980), and minor or unpublished sites such as Hartshill (C. Hart, pers. comm.). Final, definitive reports are not yet available for any of these sites.

As yet there is little, if any, evidence of an indigenous Iron Age tradition of dispersed rural settlement in the Peak. Hodges' and Wildgoose's (1980) hypothesis of early second century colonisation of the area, perhaps stimulated by the development of the lead/silver industry, appears to be supported by the general second to third/fourth century date of surface sherd collections and by the second century foundation dates suggested on the basis of excavations for Roystone Grange settlement and the more sophisticated settlement at Carsington (Branigan 1985). Excavations at Staden may hint at a somewhat earlier foundation (Makepeace 1983, 1987, 1989), which may well relate to its proximity to the spa at Buxton. Few of the open settlements seem to survive into the fourth century in the Peak, although Roystone did and Carsington on the southern fringe of the area was certainly occupied through most of the fourth century (Branigan 1985; Branigan, Housley and Housley 1986). Of the larger, nucleated, settlements Buxton probably survived into the fourth century (Hart 1981, 94) but the vici at Brough and Melandra had been abandoned (Dearne 1991).

The evidence from Peak District caves is very much in accordance with the view of a second century colonisation, and indeed itself serves as a significant additional source of support for the hypothesis. Peak District caves, as we have seen, are most commonly in use in the second century and frequently appear to be fulfilling domestic (and workshop), shelter, hideaway, and burial functions. It is possible that some caves were first utilised in the late first century, but the evidence is principally from the odd coin or brooch which may have been in circulation for some decades before loss. Most of the caves continue in use to the end of the second century and several certainly or possibly run well into the third century. Usage, except at a few hideaway and shelter sites, is not indicated in the fourth century. Thus, cave and open site usage appear to follow an identical pattern in the Peak.

The caves of northern England divide into two main groups, that of the Craven area and that further west on the Lancashire/Cumbria border. The latter includes few sites occupied over any length of time, and it is on the Settle group that we can most usefully concentrate. The Romano-British use of caves in the Craven area has long attracted attention, and open settlement was first examined by Raistrick (1939) and more recently by King (1986). Raistrick concluded that both isolated homesteads and 'villages' of varying size were present in the area, and that their occupation was predominantly late first/second century and fourth century (1939, 143ff). King agrees that 'the majority of excavated settlements can be dated to the second or fourth centuries' (1986, 186) but suggests there may have been an hiatus in the middle of the second century. Whether the quantity and quality of the evidence allows us to identify such an hiatus is doubtful. Cave occupation in the Craven area appears to follow the same pattern, and to have begun in the late first century and then continued through the second and third centuries and into the fourth.

In the Mendips and the immediately surrounding area the pattern of rural settlement is more varied than in the Peak and the Craven area, for here we find well defined villages (e.g. Catsgore) as well as farmsteads (e.g. Butcombe and Bradley Hill), small towns with industrial (Charterhouse), and manufacturing (Camerton) functions, and many villas. The early development of the silver/lead mines on Mendip meant an early foundation for Charterhouse, and Camerton saw its first timber buildings perhaps in the late first century, and its masonry structures from the mid-late second century (Burnham and Wacher 1990, 295). Some of the farmsteads and villages were also established in the late first century, although the most comprehensively excavated examples, at Butcombe and Catsgore respectively, both saw very extensive remodelling in the late third century (Fowler 1968; Leech 1981). This seems to coincide with a major period of villa construction in the Mendips and to the north, whilst to the south the villa estates seem to first blossom in the early third century (Branigan 1976, 40–42).

Cave utilisation in the Mendip area seems to relate mainly to the late Roman period and to coincide with the other evidence for increased rural settlement and activity. Apart from a little occasional shelter usage only Wookey Hole shows any clear evidence of earlier use, and this may have been mainly for burials associated with the open site at Hole Ground Buildings (Ashworth and Crampton 1964).

The caves of south Wales are mainly concentrated in the Gower or further west, and therefore probably lay in the territory of the Demetae. Many rural settlements here appear to represent a degree of continuity from the Iron Age, even if the Iron Age phases are difficult to pin down because of a paucity of pottery, or even an aceramic culture (James and Williams 1982, 279f, 298). Rectangular stone-founded buildings appear to represent the impact of Romano-British culture, but they are normally found within sub-circular enclosures which are part of the native tradition. Dating evidence is slender in many cases, but such settlements appear to cover the first to fourth centuries. How relevant these settlements are to the main group of utilised caves along the coast of the Gower is debateable, for to date there is very little evidence of Romano-British settlement on the Gower apart from that provided by the caves. As we noted in chapter four, all the caves of south Wales with reasonably dated assemblages appear to have two periods of usage – late first/second and later third/fourth century – which do not appear to match any clear chronological pattern in the general development of rural settlement in the region.

Cave Usage and Cave Users in the Market Economy

Given the location of most of the caves in our catalogue of sites, well away from substantial Romano-British towns and for the most part in regions of the province which are not noted for their high level of Romanisation, we should not expect cave usage to be much involved with either the market economy or the use of money in that economy.

By and large this proves to be the case. The vast majority of caves have yielded assemblages which include only a handful of coins, bronze trinkets and fine-ware pottery vessels. Although almost half of the caves in the gazetteer have yielded coins, only twenty-one have produced more than five, and only ten have more than ten coins. These figures exclude five caves which have yielded hoards. Although such hoards suggest that people living within reasonable distance of the cave were involved in monetary transactions, they obviously contribute nothing to our understanding of the extent to which the mainstream of cave usage in Roman Britain was involved in such matters.

The same must be said of the evidence from White Woman's Hole (S25) and probably of Rowberrow (S19) for counterfeiting. This is an interesting sidelight on the use of caves for activities very directly related to the money economy, but it remains no more than a sidelight.

It is impossible to make any meaningful comparisons between the number of coins found in caves with those found on open sites but a glance at the villa coin lists randomly collected together by Reece (1989, 35) immediately makes the point that by and large villas and caves are in different leagues when it comes to coin loss (and presumably, therefore, coin usage). Only Long Hole, Cheddar (S10) and Wookey Hole nearby (S26) offer any broadly comparative coin lists, with 375+ and 134+ coins respectively. These, with their heavy bias towards later fourth century issues, fall clearly into Reece's pattern of rural coin loss (1989, 38–9), as one might expect. Within the pattern of rural coin loss, however, they do stand out as having unusually high numbers of coins. Long Hole betters the score of all but three of Reece's selection of twenty-four villas and Wookey Hole would be in the top half of the list.

If one turns to other types of rural settlement in south-west England then the coin losses at Cheddar and Wookey look even more substantial. Whilst the six coins from the Romano-British farmstead at Brockworth near Gloucester (Rawes 1981, 69) is an exceptionally low number, the coins from the much closer farmsteads at Butcombe and Bradley Hill, both of which sites were extensively excavated, should provide a fair comparison with Cheddar and Wookey. Butcombe yielded 27 coins (Fowler 1968, 1970) and Bradley Hill 69 (Leech 1981, 207: we exclude the foundation hoard of 9 coins since we have excluded hoards from both Cheddar and Wookey from our totals).

Although these must be very crude comparisons, both Long Hole, Cheddar and Wookey Hole do appear to be 'rich' in coin loss, and much closer to the sort of quantities which seem normal in villas than on lower status rural farming settlements. We might explore this situation further by comparing the quantity and variety of bronzework from these sites.

Fulford (1982, 414–6) noted that urban sites appear to have a greater quantity and variety of bronzework than rural ones, even where the rural sites are villas, and that this may relate either to a greater concentration of craftsmen in the towns or greater consumer demand for fine bronzework there. If we tabulate coins, bronze objects and types of bronze object from our two caves and two nearby open sites we certainly find that the caves better the open sites in all three categories:

	Number Coins	Number Bronzes	Types Bronzes
Wookey Hole	375+	36	13
Long Hole, Cheddar	134+	27	9
Bradley Hill	69	12	6
Butcombe	27	11	4

(The totals include fragmentary items but not pieces of embellishment such as sheathing and binding).

Interestingly, the open sites which provide the closest parallels to Wookey Hole (and to a lesser extent Long Hole) in this respect are two other nearby settlements, Catsgore and Ilchester. Catsgore is a village site, extensively explored and published by Leech (1982) and Ilchester is of course a small town, where extensive excavations, mainly extra-mural, took place in 1974–5 (Leach 1982). The bald 'statistics' of these two sites are:

	Number Coins	Number Bronzes	Types Bronzes
Ilchester	370	143	17
Catsgore	437	78	13

(The Catsgore coin total excludes two small hoards, since hoards are excluded from Wookey, Long Hole, and Bradley Hill figures above).

49

Given all the problems of comparing these assemblages, it still seems that the users of Wookey Hole and Long Hole might be deemed to have tastes and/or purchasing power that was more akin to the villagers of Catsgore and the townspeople of Ilchester than the farmers of Butcombe and Bradley Hill.

One specific group of bronzework which may emphasise the common tastes of the inhabitants of Ilchester, Catsgore, Wookey and Long Hole – and also sets them apart from Butcombe and Bradley Hill – is toilet equipment. Manicure implements are absent at Butcombe and Bradley Hill and are rarely found on lower status 'native' farmsteads. Although a handful appear with other Roman products as luxury imports before the invasion, they are essentially a Roman introduction to Britain and may be seen as a rough-and-ready guide to the adoption of Romanised personal hygiene. The village of Catsgore yielded three such items, and the small town of Ilchester produced six; bearing in mind the small population of the caves the four from Wookey and the one from Long Hole may be regarded as significant. Although these variations in the frequency of coins, bronzes, types of bronzes, and toilet implements may all be dismissed as of uncertain significance due to the uncontrolled variables in their survival and recovery, all four groups of material point to the same conclusion and collectively carry some weight. The cave users of Wookey and Long Hole seem to share the material culture and tastes of the nucleated populations of Catsgore and Ilchester.

It is possible that this is related to the workshop/craft activities of Wookey and possibly of Long Hole (supra p.23). Amongst the finds from Long Hole are two steelyard arms, which are strange things to find in a domestic cave occupation and are more likely to be associated with some sort of commercial activity. Of the four open sites in this area which we have been using for comparative purposes, only the small town of Ilchester yields even a single balance arm.

The connection between workshop usage of caves and Romanised behaviour is also suggested by the evidence from caves in other regions. There are few civilian towns and few villas in the Peak District, and the Settle area of Yorkshire, so that comparisons in both areas are difficult.

There are far fewer coins on civilian sites in the Peak District and the North than there are in the south and east, so that the relatively small numbers of coins from Poole's Cavern (19+), Thirst House (9), and Victoria and Albert Caves (31+) cannot be compared with the Somerset sites discussed above. They are, however, amongst the most prolific ten cave sites in terms of coinage, and share with Wookey and Long Hole a quantity and variety of bronzework and a preference for toilet implements unusual on lower status sites (Figure 5.1). The finds from these workshop sites can be summarised thus:

	Number Bronzes	Types Bronzes	Toilet Items
Poole's Cavern	119	11	4
Thirst House	56	11	5
Victoria/Albert	80+	12	3

In these instances, where we believe that the workshop activity was bronze-working, producing jewellery and other items for the market-place, both the quantity and the variety of bronzework encountered presumably reflect the tastes of the market for which they were intended, rather than those of the producers. They testify, nevertheless, to the relationship which existed between the cave users and the settlements where their markets were to be found. In this context these three caves are also interesting in that they have each produced a little evidence for involvement in written transactions of some sort, with seal boxes from Victoria and Albert and Thirst House, and a stylus from Poole's Cavern. These again would point to activities related to higher status sites, be they towns or forts.

Where then were the markets for these cave-using craftsmen? The finds at Peak District and Craven cave sites indicate that the products of the craftsmen included a variety of jewellery and other decorative metalwork items amongst which brooches are fairly conspicuous. A number of these may be regarded as essentially 'native' products, or at least products displaying native features. These include trumpet brooches, many with late Celtic relief decoration (Figure 5.2), plate headed brooches (which may have developed from them), S-shaped solid and wire brooches, enamelled and un-enamelled dragonesque brooches, penannular brooches, button-and-loop fasteners, and items decorated in late Celtic styles such as the belt plate from Thirst House and the Dolphin mount from Poole's Cavern. Indeed as Allason-Jones (1989, 17) has pointed out, enamelling – prominently and much used on the finds from the Craven and Peak District – was very much a Celtic skill.

Whilst the workshop assemblages also contain more Romanised products such as manicure sets there is in general a 'native' character to much of the assemblages; even on the Thirst House manicure set we see opposed trumpets, characteristic of Celtic styles (Figure 5.2). This may be significant for Allason-Jones (1989, 19) has concluded from a study of native types of find from Roman military sites, in comparison to the paucity of Romanised objects on native sites north of Hadrian's Wall, that in the earlier empire native craftsmen in the Wall region were finding significant markets amongst the military for native, and to the troops novel, items. Thus in particular she points to enamelled dragonesque brooches which may have appealed to 'the gaudy taste of the military', and to trumpet brooches, much favoured by the military but with the quality of the late Celtic scrollwork deteriorating due to large scale production (Allason-Jones 1989, 17). Cave workshops in the Craven district and the Peak might therefore have found markets in the Pennine forts, particularly in the later first and second century. Some of the products could have travelled further afield to small towns and vici around the fringes of the southern Pennines such as Aldborough, Castleford, Doncaster, Littlechester and Manchester. In the case of Poole's Cavern and Thirst House, however, it is hard to believe that the prime market was not the spa centre at Buxton. The military and civilian clientele of a spa such as Buxton would have been a good market for high quality bronze jewellery and even more so for superb manicure sets like those found in Poole's Cavern and Thirst House.

Cave Usage and the Rural Economy

The majority of the caves utilised during the Romano-British period can have few direct relationships with urban settlements. They were mostly appendages of open-air rural settlements, for whom they served as places of temporary shelter or burial, and in a few cases perhaps as seasonal alternatives. Many of the caves identified as hideaways were probably also utilised in this way by persons from nearby open-air settlements, although a few may have been chosen deliberately for their isolation from all places of permanent habitation.

In seeking to document and more closely examine the links between caves and open-air rural settlement we have sought to use analytical studies of both metalwork and pottery but with little success. This was not unexpected, but pilot programmes of analysis were nevertheless tried since it was felt that although it might prove impossible to firmly document links it might be possible to demonstrate the absence of relationships in some cases.

In the case of metalwork the analyses were hampered by the obvious reluctance of museum curators to allow even very small samples to be taken from their best exhibits. Thus, analyses were for the most part conducted on fragmentary items of no great distinction, whereas ideally they would be conducted on, for example, some of the finest fibulae. The programme was undertaken by M. C. Bishop and M. J. Dobby, to whom we are grateful for permission to publish their results. Eleven items were analysed, coming from Poole's Cavern (7), Thirst House (2), Thors Fissure (1) and Reynard's Cave (1). This is by no means an ideal sample, since the small number of samples overall and the one or two only from three of the caves obviously make any valid comparison of the metallurgy at these sites impossible. All that can be said is that the metallurgy of all the samples seems very similar, with the exception of samples 1 (from Reynard's Cave) and 6 (from Poole's Cavern). The metalworkers at Poole's Cavern and Thirst House, were both working mainly in tin-bronze. If this was true of the brooches from Thirst House as well as the two items analysed, then this would repeat the picture of brooch production at Poole's Cavern which Bayley has demonstrated was mainly in bronze and gunmetal (Branigan and Bayley 1989, 44–5). Poole's Cavern seems to be out of step with the mainstream of Romano-British brooch metallurgy (which favoured leaded bronzes), and the very limited evidence from Thirst House and Thors Fissure suggests this may be true of Peak District metallurgy in general.

The sample used for pottery analysis was more satisfactory, comprising a selected group of twenty-nine sherds from the pottery assemblages from three cave sites and four open sites. The object of the exercise was to see to what extent cave and open sites were obtaining their coarse wares from the same sources. Our sherd sample therefore concentrated on orange wares and grey wares; fine wares were deliberately excluded from consideration as was Derbyshire Ware. Examples of different fabrics within each of the two groups of ware were selected for thin-sectioning. Poole's Cavern provided three samples of different grey wares and three of orange, Thirst House supplied just one of each, and Frank i'th' Rocks just a single sample of grey ware. The number of different fabrics available for sampling reflects principally the size of the surviving pottery assemblage from each site. Open sites sampled included Buxton Spa (two grey and two orange), Buxton Silverlands (one grey and one orange), Staden settlement (two grey and two orange) and Brough vicus (five grey and five orange). The examination of the thin-sections was not undertaken to identify the source from which the various fabrics were obtained, but simply to see to what extent the fabrics used at the caves and open sites were identical or different, thereby indicating whether or not the same market centres or potteries were utilised.

The programme was carried out by Dr P. Nicholson, to whom we are indebted for permission to publish his results. The orange wares proved a very varied lot of fabrics, not easily grouped. All the sites except Brough, however, produced grey fabrics which fell into a single group. The sherds from Brough, although the biggest sample, "share similarities with the other 6 sites, but they are more similar to each other than to these" (Nicholson, unpub. report). These results seem to suggest that the settlements in and around Buxton, including the caves, probably all obtained much of their coarse wares from a similar market (presumably Buxton itself) but that Brough obtained its supplies elsewhere. It is possible that this difference might reflect the role played by agents purchasing in bulk for military posts in the area, as much as the economics of supply to

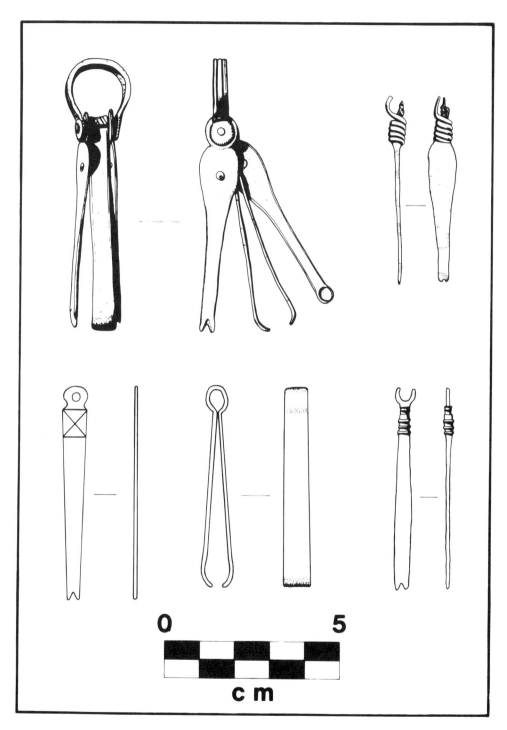

Figure 5.1   Toilet implements from Peak District caves, Derbyshire.

the fort at Brough.

Whilst these results are unsurprising, they perhaps serve to emphasise that the bulk of cave usage in Roman Britain occurred within the network of economic and social relationships which bound urban and rural communities together. With the exception of some of the 'hideaways', cave usage formed part of the normal pattern of settlement and land use in those areas where caves are to be found. Exactly how the caves' usage related to the open rural settlements is difficult to determine for the reasons given earlier in this chapter, but we can perhaps approach this question by a brief examination of cave and open site juxtapositions in the Peak District.

Two of our burial caves, Fox Hole (P16) and Frank i'th' Rocks (P17), can plausibly be related to nearby Romano-British settlement sites. Less than 400m from Fox Hole is an enclosure and fields on Wheeldon Hill, discovered by Makepeace (1985). Another settlement site recorded by Makepeace at the foot of Wolfscote Hill is separated from the cemetery in Frank i'th' Rocks by less than 300m and the River Dove. A second settlement, with terraced platforms and fields, is situated 800m ESE of Frank i'th' Rocks at Wolfscote Grange (Makepeace 1985, 131, figure 44), and although this overlooks the cave site from a height of more than 300m its occupiers could equally well have been the contributing population for the cemetery.

If, as we suggested above, metalworking associated with domestic occupation of caves was particularly appropriate in the winter months, then we might seek nearby open settlements to pair with Poole's Cavern and Thirst House. Less than a kilometre to the east of Thirst House (P28) is the nucleated settlement of The Burrs (Figure 5.3), with several enclosures and houses (Makepeace 1985, 153, figure 42; Hart 1981, figure 8, 11); traces of field systems survive nearby and also on the opposite (west) side of Deep Dale. The community at The Burrs would certainly have been aware of Thirst House cave and a seasonal use of the cave for metalworking can be most economically related to that settlement. On present evidence Poole's Cavern (P23) has no open settlement within a kilometre, but the area immediately north-west of it is totally obscured by the suburbs of Buxton. The settlement at Staden, excavated by Makepeace, is over 2km east of Poole's Cavern, but it serves along with The Burrs and other possible settlement sites in the immediate area, to suggest the sort of settlements which were strung along the high ground south of the Wye and may have extended as far west as the area around Poole's Cavern.

Caves which appear to have been utilised only for occasional usage cannot so easily be assumed to relate to their nearest contemporary open settlements, since the proximity of the home base would seem to obviate the need for temporary shelter in the cave in many instances, unless perhaps they were used for occupation in exceptionally bad weather. Churn Hole (P5), for example, may have served as a useful shelter point half way between the settlement at Dimin Dale and the higher pastures around High Low. Dimin Dale was excavated by Major Harris, and is also recorded by Makepeace (1985, 136, figure 47). A sub-triangular enclosure, house-sites, and fields are noted and there is much Romano-British pottery from the area, including samian and colour-coated.

The cave at Ravencliffe (P25), on the other hand, is not so easily seen as a temporary shelter for shepherds living in the settlement at Hay Top (Makepeace 1985, 145).They are only about half a kilometre apart and at more or less the same altitude. If anything it is easier to envisage Ravencliffe acting as a hideaway site for people from Hay Top, near enough to be quickly reached in time of emergency but also well hidden. There is, of course, a third possibility which is that use of Ravencliffe for occasional shelter might in any case pre-date the occupation of the Hay Top settlement. In that event, its value as a temporary refuge for shepherds in this area is

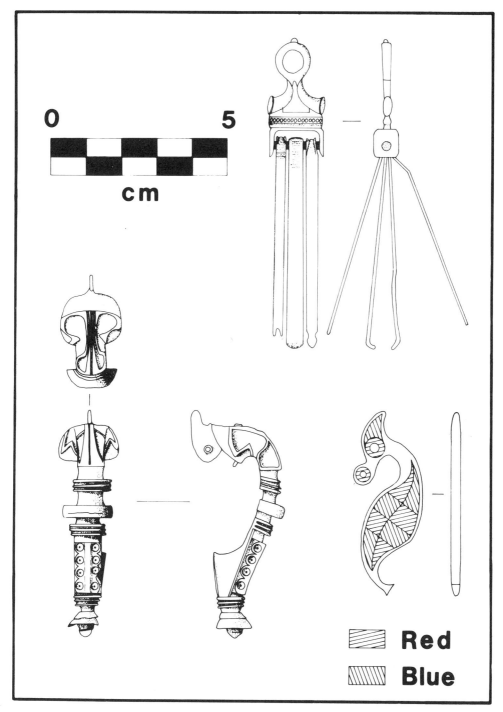

Figure 5.2   Bronze toiletry set, late Celtic decorated Trumpet Brooch, and an enameled dragonesque brooch, Thirst House Cave, Derbyshire.

more easily understood.

As for hideaway caves, Reynard's Cave (P26) in Dove Dale may provide a good example, being able to serve as a safe place for occupants of the open settlement at Thorpe Pasture, about one and a half kilometres to the south-east (Makepeace 1985, 130). The quantity of pottery found in the cave, apparently spread over a period of one to two centuries, suggests intermittent use over a long period of time. Some of the usage may have been for occasional shelter rather than as a refuge, but the cave's location does not lend itself so easily to that usage. Old Woman's House (P20) is also an interesting example of a hideaway cave, for it is almost equidistant from the Dimin Dale open settlement with Churn Hole, but whereas the location and nature of the latter suggests it could have been used for occasional shelter by shepherds, Old Woman's House provided a bolt hole if needed. That is, the two caves may have played complimentary roles in serving the open settlement.

Finally we should give special attention to the caves around Wetton in the Manifold valley. The nine caves in this complex appear to have met a variety of complementary needs. Thors Cave (P29) and Elderbush Cave (P14) seem to have functioned as domestic occupation sites, and there is some evidence for workshop activity in Elderbush. On the available evidence they were probably in contemporary occupation in the middle and late second century, although use of Elderbush may have begun later and ended later than that of Thors Cave. Beeston Tor Cave (P3) and Seven Ways Cave (P27) were most likely used for occasional shelter, though Seven Ways is so close to Elderbush and Thors Cave that it might more plausibly be interpreted as a supplementary storage space for the domestic occupations there. Five small caves in the vicinity are identified by us as most probably hideaways. Cheshire Wood Cave (P4) and Darfur Ridge Cave (P11) cannot be dated more narrowly than 'RB' but Thors Fissure (P30), Ossums Crag Cave (P21) and Ossums Eyrie (P22) all seem to have been utilised in the second century.

There are traces of fields in the area above Beeston Tor Cave, but by far the most important open settlement seems to have been that at Borough Holes, excavated in the mid nineteenth century. It is clear from the accounts which survive of this site (Bateman 1861) that it was an extensive and organised settlement of huts with limestone slab flooring. Along with much pottery were found several iron knives and tools, some lead ore, iron and bronze fibulae and animal bones. There were also at least three coins, two of the late third century and one of the mid-fourth. It is tempting to see the nine caves nearby serving supplementary functions to this open site.

On present evidence, however, we should not too readily accept this interpretation, since there is no clear evidence of second century occupation of the Borough Hole settlement and the evidence from the caves is heavily weighted towards the earlier Roman period. The alternative scenario is that in the second century, Romano-British occupation in this part of the Manifold valley was actually focussed in the caves, which between them provided the secure base from which the fields and pastures around could be exploited. The foundation of a large open settlement may come later, and the settlement may have largely replaced the cave usage. The Manifold valley may be an unusual example where cave usage was not functionally complementary to open settlement occupation, but rather preceded it.

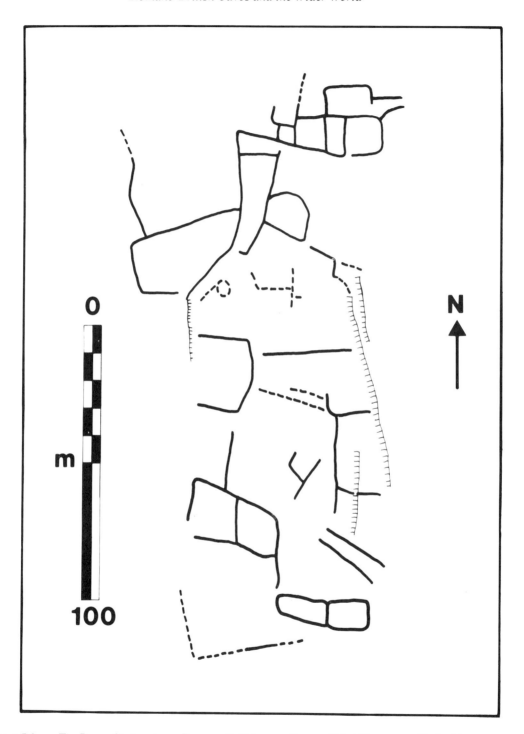

Figure 5.3   The Burrs, Chelmorten; a Romano-British open site near Thirst House cave, Derbyshire.

Conclusion

In the preceding pages of this monograph we have seen that most areas in England and Wales which have caves reveal some evidence for their utilisation in the Roman period. Their use has been seen to extend, in general terms, from soon after the conquest to the later fourth century, although few individual caves show evidence for even episodic use throughout that period of time. Only a handful of caves might be even tentatively proposed as examples of continuity from the Iron Age to the Roman period, and even fewer hint at continuity of usage into the Post-Roman era. By and large then, the reasons why caves were used in the Romano-British period was for their particular value and utility at the time rather than as part of an on-going rural tradition in certain parts of the country. The only exception to that might be the use of caves for burials, which accounts for about twenty percent of all Romano-British cave usage. Of the other uses to which caves were put in the Roman period the most common (at least a third) was occasional shelter. Use as hideaways and as a place of domestic occupation each accounted for about twenty percent of cave usage; domestic usage included five examples where we believe a workshop also existed. Somewhat surprisingly only one cave was thought to possibly have been used as a shrine.

As far as one can tell from the often inadequate chronological evidence from the caves, cave usage was generally contemporary with the occupation of open sites in the same regions, although there are some interesting regional variations in the chronological pattern of cave usage. These were discussed in chapter four, and they might repay further study and consideration in the future. There can be little doubt that most cave usage was directly related to the occupation of open settlements and that the caves served various ancillary functions for those sites. The few caves which do not necessarily reflect that pattern are the handful which we have identified as workshop sites. As we saw, there are some reasons for thinking that these caves related more directly with nucleated settlements, be they small towns, forts or vici. Certainly the evidence from these caves gives the lie to any suggestion that cave usage in the Romano-British period was confined to vagabonds, fugitives or homeless peasants. Some caves were clearly used by fugitives and others served as temporary shelter for a wide range of country-dwellers and travellers; most were probably part of the mainstream pattern of rural settlement and land use in those areas where caves are common. A few were apparently the home of skilled and successful craftsmen.

Bibliography

Allason-Jones, L. (1989). 'Introductory Remarks on Native and Roman Trade in the North of Britain', in: Van Driel-Murray, C. (ed) *Roman Military Equipment: The Sources of the Evidence* British Archaeological Reports, International Series 476, Oxford.

Ashworth, H. and Crampton, D. (1964). 'Hole Ground Roman Buildings, Wookey Hole', *Wells Natural History and Archaeological Society Report* 7:5.

Barret, J.H. and Boon, G. (1972). 'A Roman Counterfeiters' Den', *Proceedings of the University of Bristol Speleological Society* 13.1:61–82.

Bateman, T. (1861). *Ten Years Diggings.* J.R.Smith, London and W. Bembrose, Derby.

Bestwick, P. and Merrills, D. (1983) 'L.H. Butcher's Survey of Early Settlements and Fields in the South Pennines', *Hunter Society Transactions* 12:16–50.

Binford, L. (1983) *In Pursuit of the Past.* Thames and Hudson, London.

Blackman, D. and Branigan, K. (1977). 'An Archaeological Survey of the Lower Catchment of the Ayiofarango Valley', *Annual of the British School at Athens* 72:13–84.

Boon, G. and Rahtz, P. (1966). 'Third Century Counterfeiting at Whitchurch, Soms.', *Archaeological Journal* 122:13–51.

Bramwell, D. (1958) 'Final Excavation Report on Ossums Eyrie Cave' *Peakland Archaeological Soc. Newsletter* 15,8.

Bramwell, D. et al (1983). 'Excavations at Poole's Cavern, Buxton: An Interim Report', *Derbyshire Archaeological Journal* 103:47–74.

Branigan, K. (1976). *The Roman Villa in South West England*, Moonraker Press, Bradford-on-Avon.

Branigan, K. (1980). 'Villas in the North: Change in the Rural Landscape ?' In Branigan, K. (ed) *Rome and the Brigantes.* Dept. of Prehistory and Archaeology, Sheffield .

Branigan, K. (1980a). *Roman Britain*, Reader's Digest, London.

Branigan, K. (1985). 'Lutudarum', *Popular Archaeology* 6:39–41.

Branigan, K. (1991) Civilian Develoment in a Military Zone: The Peak District AD 43 – 400, in Hodges, R. and Smith, K. (eds.) *Recent Developments in the Archaeology of the Peak District.* J.R. Collis Publications, Sheffield, pp.57–67.

Branigan, K. and Bayley, J. (1989). 'The Romano-British Metalwork from Poole's Cavern, Buxton', *Derbyshire Archaeological Journal* 109:34–50.

Branigan, K. and Dearne, M.J. (1991). *A Gazetteer of Romano-British Caves and Their Finds.* Department of Archaeology and Prehistory, Sheffield.

Branigan, K. and Dearne, M.J. (1991a). 'The Small Finds from Thirst House Cave, Deepdale: A Reappraisal', In Hodges, R. and Smith, K. (eds) *Recent Developments in the Archaeology of the Peak District*, J.R. Collis Publications, Sheffield, pp.85–110.

Branigan, K.and Dearne, M.J. (forthcoming a). 'The Romano-British finds from Wookey Hole: A Reappraisal', *Proceedings of the Somerset Archaeological and Natural History Society.*

Branigan, K. and Dearne, M.J. (forthcoming b). 'Romano-British Usage of the Caves In Cheddar Gorge', *Proceedings of the University of Bristol Speleological Society.*

Branigan, K., Dearne, M.J and Rutter, J. (forthcoming). 'Romano-British Occupation of Minchin Hole Cave, Gower', *Archaeologia Cambrensis.*

Branigan, K. and Fowler, P. (1976). *The Roman West Country*, David and Charles, Newton Abbott.

Branigan, K., Housley, J. and Housley, C. (1986). 'Two Roman Lead Pigs from Carsington', *Derbyshire Archaeological Journal* 106:5–17.

Burnham, B. and Wacher, J. (1990). *The Small Towns of Romano-Britain* London. Batsford.

Davies, M. (1983). 'The Excavation of Upper Kendricks Cave, Llandudno', *Studies in Speleology* 4:45–52.

Dawkins, W.B. (1874). *Cave Hunting* Macmillan, London.

Dearne, M.J. (1990). 'Military Equipment from Romano-British Caves', *ARMA, The Newsletter of the Roman Military Equipment Conference.*

Dearne, M.J. (1991). 'The Military Vici of the South Pennines: Retrospect and Prospect', In Hodges, R. and Smith, K. (eds) *Recent Developments in the Archaeology of the Peak District*, J.R. Collis Publications, Sheffield, pp.69–84.

Dobson, D.P. (1931). *The Archaeology of Somerset*, Methuen, London.

Edward, R. (1793). A Description of the County of Angus in 1678. T. Colville, Dundee.

Elkington, D. (1976). 'The Mendip Lead Industry', In Branigan, K. and Fowler, P. (eds) *The Roman West Country*, David and Charles, Newton Abbot, pp.183–97.

Fowler, P. (1968). 'Excavations of a Romano-British Settlement at Row of Ashes Farm, Butcombe', *Proceedings of the University of* Bristol *Speleological Society* 11:209–36.

Fowler, P. (1970). 'The Iron Age', In Campbell, J. *et al. The Mendip Hills in Prehistoric and Roman Times Bristol*, Bristol Archaeological Research Group, pp.17–23.

Fowler, P. (1970a). 'Fieldwork and Excavation in the Butcombe Area', *Proceedings of the University of Bristol Speleological Society* 12:169–94.

Fowler, P. (1976). 'Farms and Fields in the Roman West Country' in: Branigan, K.and Fowler, P. (eds) *The Roman West Country*, David and Charles, Newton Abbot, pp.162–82.

Frere, S.S. (1987). *Britannia* (3rd Edition) Routledge, London.

Fulford, M. (1982). 'Town and Country in Roman Britain – a Parasitical Relationship ?', In: Miles, D. (ed) *The Romano-British Countryside*, British Archaeological Reports, Oxford, pp.403–20.

Gentles, D. (1984). *Troglodytes and Pyromaniacs: Present and Palaeolithic* Unpublished B.A. Dissertation, University of Sheffield.

Gentles, D. and Smithson, P. (1986). 'Fires in Caves: Effects on Temperature and Airflow', *Proceedings of the University of Bristol Speleological Society* 17:205–17.

Gilks, J. (1989). 'Cave Burials of Northern England', *British Archaeology* 11:11–15.

Hawkes, C.J., Rogers, J.M. and Tratmanm, E.K. (1978) 'Romano-British Cemetery in the Fourth Chamber of Wookey Hole Cave, Somerset' *Proc. University of Bristol Speleological Soc.* 15:23–52.

Hart, C. (1981). *The North Derbyshire Archaeological Survey to AD 1500* Chesterfield (NDAT).

Hartley, B. and Fitts, L. (1988). *The Brigantes* Gloucester (Alan Sutton).

Hodges, R. and Wildgoose, M. (1980). 'Roman or Native in the White Peak' in: Branigan, K. (ed) *Rome and the Brigantes*, Dept of Prehistory and Archaeology, Sheffield, pp.48–53.

Hussey, M. (1966). 'Final Excavations at the Lesser Garth Cave', *Transactions of the Cardiff Naturalists Society* 93:18–39.

James, H. and Williams, G. (1982). 'Rural Settlement in Roman Dyfed' in: Miles, D. (ed) *The Romano-British Countryside*, British Archaeological Reports, Oxford, pp.289–312.

Kempe, D. (1988). *Living Underground*, The Herbert Press, London.

King, A. (1986). 'Romano-British Farms and Farmers in Craven, N. Yorkshire', In Manby, T. and Turnbull, P. (eds) *Archaeology in the Pennines*, British Archaeological Reports, Oxford, pp.181–93.

Leach, P. (1982). *Ilchester Vol. I: Excavations 1974-5*, Western Archaeological Trust, Bristol.

Leech, R. (1976). 'The Larger Agricultural Settlements in the West Country' in: Branigan, K. and Fowler, P. (eds) *The Roman West Country*, David and Charles, Newton Abbot, pp.142–61.

Leech, R. (1981). 'The Excavation of a Romano-British Farmstead and Cemetery on Bradley Hill, Somerset' *Britannia* 12:177–252.

Leech, R. (1982). *Excavations at Catsgore 1970-73* Western Archaeological Trust, Bristol .

Leitch, R. (1987) 'Green Bottle Howffs: A Pilot Study of Inhabited Caves' *Vernacular Building* 11:15–20.

Makepeace, G. (1983). 'A Romano-British Settlement at Staden, near Buxton', *Derbyshire Archaeological Journal* 103:75–85.

Makepeace, G. (1985). *A Geographical and Systematic Analysis of the Later Prehistoric and Romano-British Settlement of the Upland Limestone and Gritstone Margins of the Peak District and North-East Staffordshire*, Unpublished M.A. Thesis, University of Keele.

Makepeace, G. (1987). 'The Romano-British Settlement at Standen near Buxton: The 1983 Excavations', *Derbyshire Archaeological Journal* 107:24–34.

Makepeace, G. (1989). 'The Romano-British Settlement at Staden near Buxton: The 1984 and 1985/86 Excavations', *Derbyshire Archaeological Journal* 109:17–33.

Martin, A. (1984). *Kintyre: The Hidden Past*, John Donald, Edinburgh.

Raistrick, A. (1939). 'Iron Age Settlements in West Yorkshire', *Yorkshire Archaeological Journal* 34:115–51.

Rawes, B. (1981). 'The Romano-British site at Brockworth, Glos.', *Britannia* 12:45–78.

Reece, R. (1989). 'Coins and Villas' in: Branigan, K. and Miles, D. (eds) *The Economies of Romano-British Villas*, Dept. of Archaeology and Prehistory, Sheffield, pp.34–41.

Ross, A. (1974). *Pagan Celtic Britain*, Cardinal, London.

Sanderson, S. (1957). 'A Packman's Bivvy in Moidart', *Scottish Studies* 1:243–5.

Shaw, L. (1882). *The History of the Province of Moray* Vol.2, Hamilton Adams, London.

Smith, C. (1986). *Mid-Argyll Cave and Rock Shelter Survey* No.2, Dept of Archaeology, Newcastle-upon-Tyne.

Smith, C. (1988). *Mid-Argyll Cave and Rock Shelter Survey* No.4, Dept of Archaeology, Newcastle-upon-Tyne.

Smith, C. (forthcoming). 'The Use of Caves or the Ballad of Sawney Bean', *Scottish Archaeological Review*.

Smithson, P. (1982). 'Temperature Variation in Cresswell Crags Caves' *East Midland Geography* 8:51–64.

Smithson, P. (1986). 'Cave Climate at Cresswell' In Jenkinson, R. and Gilbertson, D. *Robin Hood's Cave: Quaternary Geology and Archaeology*. Dept of Archaeology and Prehistory, Sheffield .

Smithson, P. (1991) 'Interrelationships between Cave and Outside Temperatures in the Peak District of Derbyshire' *Theoretical and Applied Climatology 44, 65–73*.

Smithson, P. and Branigan, K. (forthcoming). 'Poole's Cavern, Buxton. A Romano-British Working Environment', *Derbyshire Archaeological Journal* .

Todd, M. (1973). *The Coritani*, Duckworth, London.

Wilson, G. (1926). *Some Caves and Crags of Peakland* W. Edmunds, Chesterfield.

Appendix 1   A List of Caves and Museums visited during the Research Programme

A. LIST OF CAVES VISITED

Derbyshire:

P7	Church Hole
P8	Pin Hole
P9	Robin Hoods Cave
P10	Mother Grundys Parlour
P13	Dowel Cave
P16	Fox Hole
P20	Old Woman's House
P23	Poole's Cavern
P25	Ravencliffe
P28	Thirst House
P29	Thors Cave

Northern England:

N2	Brides Chair
N3	Dog Holes, Wharton Crag
N7	Jubilee Cave
N18	Victoria and Albert Caves

South Wales:

W1	Bacon Hole
W12	Minchin Hole
W16	Ogof yr Esgyrn
W19	Spritsail Tor

Mendips:

S4	Badger Hole
S8	Goughs Old Cave
S9	Goughs New Cave
S10	Long Hole/Slitter
Sll	Pride Evans Hole
S26	Wookey Hole

B. LIST OF MUSEUMS VISITED

King John's Hunting Lodge, Axbridge
British Museum, London
Buxton Museum and Art Gallery
Cheddar Caves Museum and Exhibition
Derby Museum and Art Gallery
Tolson Memorial Museum, Huddersfield
Lancaster City Museum
Manchester Museum
National Museum of Wales, Cardiff
University College of Swansea & Royal Institute of South Wales Museum
Sheffield City Museum
Craven Museum, Skipton
Stoke City Museum and Art Gallery
University of Bristol Spelaeological Society Museum
Wells Museum
Woodspring Museum, Western-Super-Mare
Wookey Hole Caves and Mill

Appendix 2   The Proposed Functional Attribution of Caves used during the Romano-British Period

We list below the caves, with their regional catalogue numbers, that we identify as fulfilling each of the seven types of usage which were discussed in chapters 2 and 3.

Needless to say, many of the attributions proposed must be tentative and the degree of certainty with which attributions have been made varies considerably from one cave to another. Some of the problems which have to be faced in identifying the function(s) which a cave fulfilled are discussed at the beginning of chapter three. Nevertheless we have made a careful assessment of the evidence from each site (cave location, size, and morphology, and the size and nature of the material assemblage)in proposing our attributions and we believe that on the evidence available the attributions we propose are a 'best fit' with the models discussed in chapter 2.

A number of caves appear in two different groups, having fulfilled more than one function (sometimes concurrently, sometimes sequentially), and three caves are each listed in three different functional groups. Whilst the number of caves with evidence for Romano-British usage is 97, the total number of attributions in the following list is therefore 110. This includes seven caves for which the surviving evidence is too imprecise to allow even a tentative attribution to a group, and which are listed separately below.

DOMESTIC USAGE

Elderbush Cave (P14)
Harborough Cave (P18)
Poole's Cavern (P23)
Thirst House Cave (P28)
Thors Cave (P29)
Attermire Cave (N1)
Dowkerbottom Cave (N5)
Jubilee Cave (N7)
Greater Kelco Cave (N9)
Kinsey Cave (N13)
Sewell's Cave (N15)
Victoria & Albert Cave (N18)
Gough's Old Cave (S8)
Gough's New Cave (S9)
Long Hole (S10)
Wookey Hole (S26)
Merlins Cave (W11)
Minchin Hole (W12)
Ogof-Yr-Esgyrn (W16)

UNATTRIBUTED

Creswell Crags (unspec.) (P6)
Merlewood Cave (N14)
Spider Cave (N16)
Tom Taylors Cave (N17)
Callow Limewater Cave (S6)

WORKSHOP USAGE

Poole's Cavern (P23)
Thirst House Cave (P28)
Victoria & Albert Cave (N18)
Wookey Hole (S26)
Minchin Hole (W12)

RITUAL USAGE

Culver Hole (W3)

BURIAL USAGE

Fox Hole Cave (P16)
Frank i'th' Rocks Cave (P17)
Poole's Cavern (P23)
Thirst House (P28)
Dog Holes Cave (Warton) (N3)
Dog Holes (Haverbrack) (N4)
Fairy Hole (N6)
Backwell Cave (S3)
Charterhouse Warren Farm Swallett (S7)
Hey Wood Cave (S16)
Taylors Wood Cave (S21)
Wookey Hole (S26)
Lynx Cave (W9)
Maeshafn Cave (W10)
Merlin's Cave (W11)

Great Orme's Head Cave (W4)
Llanymynech Cave (W8)

Nant-Y-Graig (W14)
Ogof-Yr-Esgyrn (W16)
Ogof-Yr-Ychen (W17)

OCCASIONAL SHELTER USAGE

Ash Tree Cave (P1)
Beeston Tor Cave (P3)
Churn Hole (P5)
Robin Hood's Cave (P9)
Dead Man's Cave (P12)
Fissure Cave (P15)
Frank i'th' Rocks Cave (P17)
Ravencliffe Cave (P25)
Seven Ways Cave (P27)
Upper Cales Dale Cave (P31)
Wetton Mill Rock Shelter (P32)
Kirkhead Cave (N8)
Lesser Kelco Cave (N10)
Leyburn Shawl Cave (N11)
King Alfrid's Cave (N12)
Ash Hole (S2)
Badger Hole (S4)
Browne's Hole (S5)
Chelm's Combe Rock Shelter (S14)
Dinder Wood Shelter (S15)
Kents Cavern (S17)
Scragg's Hole (S20)
Tickenham Rock Shelter (S22)
Tom Tivy's Hole (S23)
Bacon Hole (W1)
B.S.Pothole (W2)
King Arthur's Cave (W5)
Lesser Garth Cave (W6)
Little Hoyle Cave (W7)
Nanna's Cave (W13)
Spritsail Tor Rock Shelter (W19)

HIDEAWAY USAGE

Bat House Cave (P2)
Cheshire Wood Cave (P4)
Darfur Ridge Cave (P11)
Dowel Cave (P13)
Dry Dale Cave (P19)
Old Woman's House Cave (P20)
Ossum's Crag Cave (P21)
Ossum's Eyrie Cave (P22)
Pymm's Parlour (P24)
Reynard's Cave (P26)
Thors Fissure Cave (P30)
Brides Chair Cave (N2)
Dog Holes (Wharton) (N3)
Anstey's Cave (S1)
Pride Evans'Hole (S11)
Soldier's Hole (S12)
Sun Hole (S13)
Little Cave, Ebbor (S18)
Rowberrow Cavern (S19)
Uphill (Quarry) Caves, No.2 (S24)
Uphill (Quarry) Caves, No.10 (S24)
White Woman's Hole (S25)
Ogof Morfran (W15)
Paviland Cave (W18)

STORAGE USE

Pin Hole Cave (P8)
Church Hole Cave (P7)
Mother Grundy's Parlour (P10)

Appendix 3   Unpublished or poorly published Romano-British Finds from Various Caves

Figure A1

Three unpublished bronze brooches from caves in Creswell Crags Gorge on the Derbyshire – Nottinghamshire border.

No. 1 is an extremely fine, fully gilded Colchester derivative fibula, perfect except for a little damage to the catch plate and one bent wing. Its highly curved, footless bow is decorated with a central plain and two beaded ridges with further mouldings at its edges. The wings have a series of ridges, one of which on each is beaded and there is beading around the margins of the spring housing. The catch plate is decorated with piercing. The way of springing the pin, simply winding it around the axis bar and tensioning it against the spring housing is unusual and may represent experimentation with types of pin springs and hinges perhaps c.55 or earlier. Certainly the general form of the brooch is early in the development of 'Dolphin' types from earlier 'Colchester' brooches. From Church Hole Cave.

No. 2 is a Hod Hill type brooch which originally had a hinged pin held on an axis bar in the rolled over top of the brooch. It is decorated with vertical beaded ribs and plain cross ribs. This type of brooch had a fairly short life from the conquest to c.65 and is quite unusual at sites as far north as this. As with the previous item is suggests usage of the caves at Cresswell soon after if not before the conquest of the area by people with Romanised tastes. From Pin Hole Cave.

No. 3 is a damaged Headstud brooch decorated with blue enamel lozenges and originally with an enamel stud. The large crest kept a wire suspension loop off of the head and the pin was hinged. There was also a stud under the foot of the brooch which may have been worn 'upside down'. The brooch reflects use of the area rather later than the preceding, either in the late first or more likely the second century. From Robin Hood's Cave.

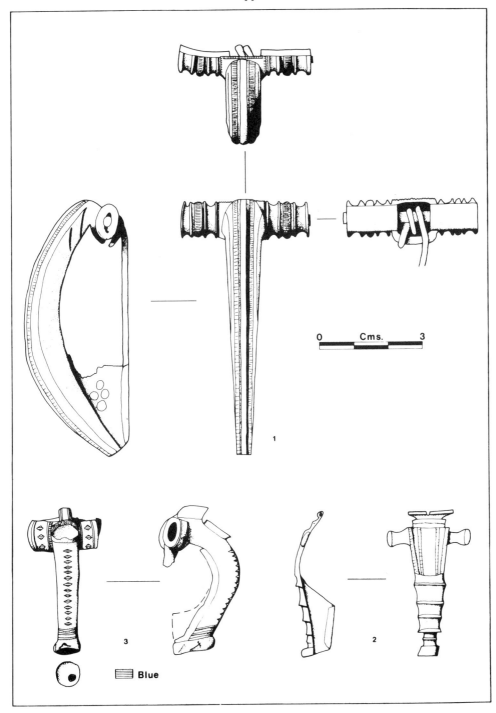

Blue

Figure A1   Three unpublished bronze brooches from caves in Cresswell Crags Gorge on the Derbyshire – Nottinghamshire border.

Figure A2

A variety of finds from caves in the Peak District.

No. 4 is a Trumpet brooch with some unusual features. A variety of broadly trumpet shaped heads are found on Trumpet brooches, but here the head is swept back far more than usual. The spring on the missing pin is also unusual in that the chord, the part of the spring tensioned against the back of the head, is above the rather than below the rest of the spring. The middle part of the bow knob is unusually large and has raised lobes at its edge with raised lozenges between. This decoration derived from the more common 'petalled' or 'acanthus' style but here has become stylised. The brooch is well-made and may reflect experimentation with the basic form in the second century. From Elderbush Cave.

No. 5 is a fairly simple bronze wire armlet. Both ends of the wire have been wound around the main part of the armlet in order to make it expandable. The cave from which this comes consists of a long, tortuous set of passages and may have been a burial site. Thus it is possible that this was buried with the deceased. From Fox Hole Cave.

   No. 6 is an unidentified object, perhaps some sort of fastening. It is a bronze bar, turned at right angles at one end with an obliquely applied, grooved head at the other end. From Frank i'th' Rocks Cave.

No. 7 is a lead weight. In form it is a faceted cone and has an iron loop set in its top with a fragment of an iron bar passing through it. Underneath the weight is recessed with a central rectangular punch mark which may have indicated its weight. It may have been used with a steelyard arm, suggesting that weighing was carried out in this cave. From Harborough Cave.

No. 8 is a gilded Polden Hill brooch. The typical features of this type of brooch are the spring with the chord held by a backward facing hook, the pierced wing ends holding its axis bar and the moulded 'appendages' where the wings and bow meet. The decoration is simple and the brooch is fairly closely dateable to c.70–90. From Old Woman's House Cave.

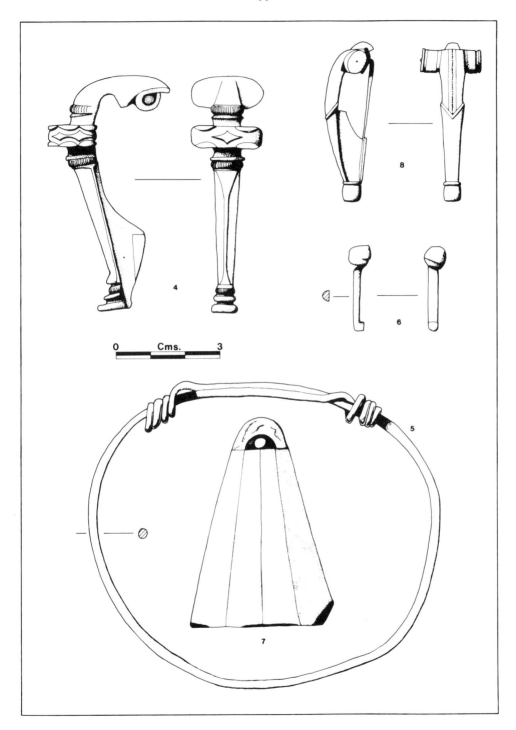

0   Cms.   3

Figure A2   A variety of finds from caves in the Peak District.

Figure A3

Contrasting pairs of finds from three Peak District Caves.

No. 9 is a Trumpet brooch from the same site as figure 2 No. 8. As well as providing a contrast in date and decorative taste to the other brooch from this site, this fibula is inherently interesting. It is one of a small group of such brooches from Derby, Manchester, Peak District caves (including figure 4 No. 16 and figure 5 No. 17) and open sites. The most notable feature of this group is the thick plate or collar behind the head. This example also has relief decoration, including 'eyes' at the top of the leg, a circular ornamented collar holding the wire suspension loop and pierced catch plate. The group may date to the early to mid second century.

Nos. 10 and 11 are a blue enamelled Knee brooch and an iron knife. They were the two main finds from a cave high in a cliff almost certainly used as a hideaway. The brooch is typical of well-made and perhaps expensive British Knee brooches with restrained decoration and dates betwen the early second and early third centuries. The knife is a fairly common, probably multipurpose type known both in the earlier Roman and preceding Iron Age periods. From Ossum's Eyrie Cave.

Nos. 12 and 13 are representatives of the two broad types of Roman brooches from the same cave. These types, the fibula or bow brooch and the penannular brooch, co-existed and both were often found in Peak District caves. Fibulae show far more variation and decoration than penannulars; this belongs to the early development of T-shaped brooches from Dolphin and Polden Hill types. It has a solid suspension loop, traces of relief decoration and may date c.80–100. Penannulars show little elaboration or variation except some decoration at the terminals and cannot be closely dated. Whilst both types fastened clothing, the former were often probably as decorative as functional. From Ravencliffe Cave.

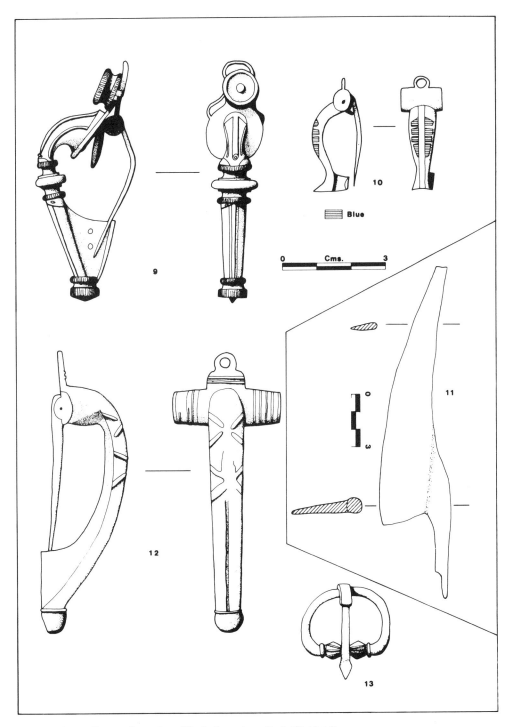

Figure A3   Contrasting pairs of finds from three Peak District Caves.

Figure A4

Various brooch types from the Manifold and Dove Valley caves of the Peak District.

No. 14 is an unusual variant of what is known as the Chester type Trumpet brooch. Its features are the sprung pin being held on an axis bar between two pierced lugs behind the head, a broad flange with integral suspension loop around the head, and a plain four element knob on the bow. In fact, this brooch represents a halfway stage between two brooch types. The top register of the bow knob here is false but probably developed from a type with lentoid mouldings at this point. Eventually all four parts of the bow knob became only flanges. Mid second century. From Reynard's Cave.

No. 15 is a badly broken but typically early brooch. Its very thin, almost undecorated, bow is undifferentiated from the broken catch plate, which was pierced. Damage prevents certain identification of how the spring was mounted, but it used a pierced lug above the head through which the chord of the spring was passed. It is likely to date 50–65 and may even have been lost before the Roman conquest of the Peak District since it comes from Thor's Cave, a large habitable site used in the Iron Age and Roman periods.

No. 16 is a Trumpet brooch belonging to the same general group as Figure 3 No. 9 and is one of two brooches again from Thor's Cave, whose similar unusual features may suggest that they came from the same workshop. These features are the step at the bottom of the catch plate, the sub-divided (here miscast) bow knob, the straight thick leg and double pierced lug spring anchorage. Here there is a large, crescentric pierced plate above the head in addition. A piece of the bow is missing. Second century, perhaps around the middle of it.

No. 17 is a Wroxeter brooch from the same site again. It developed from the Trumpet brooch and has a box-like head to hold the spring and a characteristic upper bow with vertical enamelled grooves ending in a 'tongue'. ?Later second century.

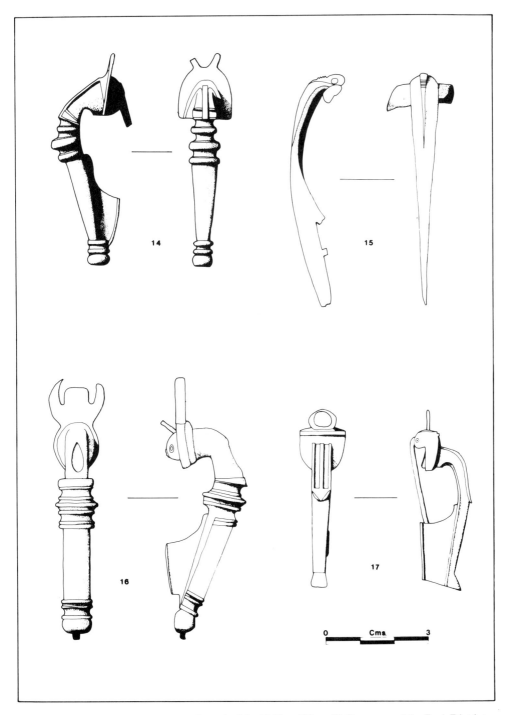

Figure A4   Various brooch types from the Manifold and Dove Valley caves of the Peak District.

Figure A5

Further brooches from Dove and Manifold Valley caves and various bronze finds from a Lancashire cave.

No. 18 is the standard unelaborated form of Trumpet brooch. It had a spring, here made of iron, hidden by a plain trumpet head and a nib on top to keep a wire suspension loop off of the head. The decoration is confined to a fairly simple three moulding foot and a stylised bow knob of petals or acanthus either side of a moulding, with further mouldings above and below. There is a piece missing from the leg of the brooch. The dating of the type is probably broad and centred on the early second century. From Thor's Cave.

No. 19 is an iron brooch with the head missing. Iron brooches are quite unusual but need not have been inferior to bronze ones. The type here is the Plate Headed brooch, a type restricted to the Peak and surrounding areas, and characterised by the highly curved bow and mid bow ornament (here lost enamel in a holder). Here there is also influence from Wroxeter brooches in the enamelled grooves. The cross hatching on the leg is unusual. From Thor's Fissure Cave and perhaps later first century.

No. 20 is a bronze balance arm with one of its two pans which were attached to either end of the arm. The pans have dot and circle ornaments in groups. Late Roman. From Dog Holes Cave, Wharton Crag.

No. 21, from the same site, is a binding of some sort, conceivably from a scabbard, ornamented with groups of incised lines. Clearly only the ornamented part was intended to be seen. A rather similar piece is known from another cave (Figure 6 No. 25) but neither are dated.

No. 22, again from the same cave but widely separated in date from No. 20, is a button and loop fastener. They were made in a number of forms and appear to have been popluar with the military, though civilians also seem to have used them. This form with triangular loop and circular (?enamelled) button was quite common up to the early second century.

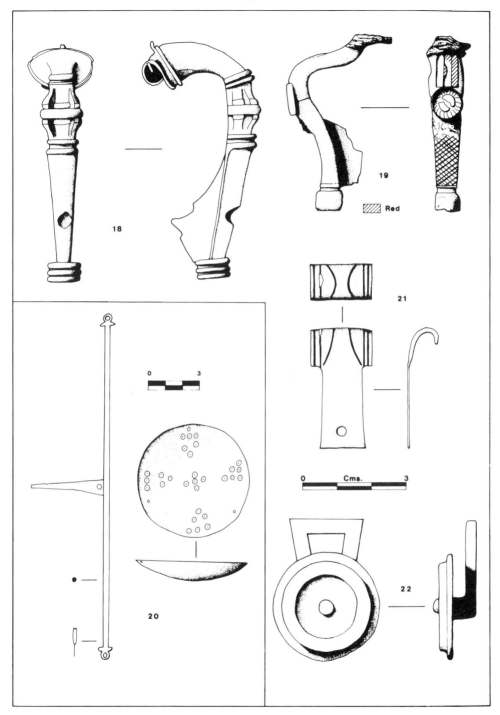

Figure A5   Further brooches from Dove and Manifold Valley caves and various bronze finds from a Lancashire cave.

Figure A6

Bronze finds from caves in the Craven area.

No. 23 is a T-shaped fibula. It has a corroded iron hinge pin, a broken suspension loop above the head and little decoration except a raised V-shaped ridge on the head. At least three other very similar brooches are known including one from Poole's Cavern, a Peak District cave, and all seem to date c.100–150. From Dowkerbottom Hole.

No. 24 is, like Figure 5 No. 22, a button and loop fastener. However this example is of an unusual design, perhaps being a one-off. The triangular lop is bent and the button is damaged but it seems that it was somewhat heart-shaped with three lobes at the top and one either side near the bottom. It has a small boss centrally. Although the design is unique, button and loop fasteners in general all seem to be second century or earlier. From Dowkerbottom Hole.

No. 25 is a decorated binding very similar to Fig. 5 No. 21 and much the same comments apply to it. Again from Dowkerbottom Hole.

No. 26 is one particularly interesting brooch from the Victoria and Albert Caves, which produced at least thirty seven fibulae of various types. This is a Headstud brooch of a rather rare type with a hole right through it to take a riveted stud (and another in the foot), a false hook at the top to keep a suspension loop off of the head and a hinged pin. However, the really unusual feature is the scroll work on the front of the the wings which curve in to the bow. These scrolls may have been enamelled. The bow has been distorted. Second century.

No. 27 is a Trumpet brooch without (very unusually) a foot, though it is possible that the foot was broken off in antiquity. It shows the pierced lug behind the head often used to hold the spring gear on Trumpet brooches and also the 'late Celtic' raised decoration seen on many of the finest brooches of the type, though (unlike Fig. 7 No. 31) it is otherwise more perfunctorily executed. Late first/early second century. From an uncertain cave in the Settle area.

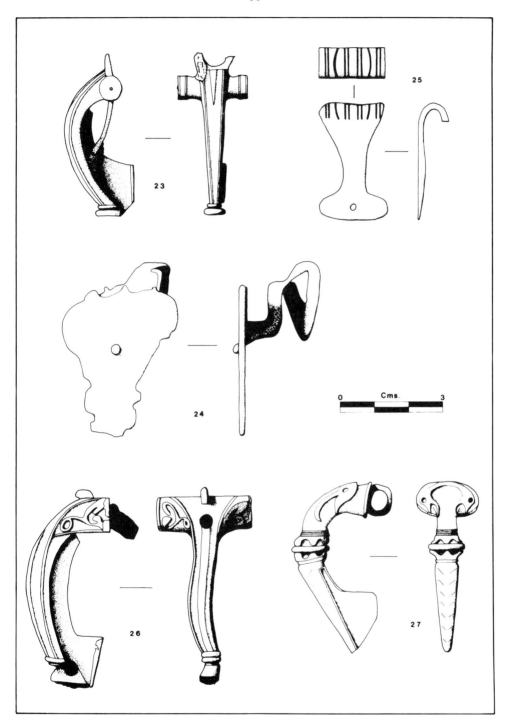

Figure A6   Bronze finds from caves in the Craven area.

Figure A7

Bronze finds from caves in the Mendips and Wales.

No. 28 is one of very few brooches from Mendip caves. It is a T-shaped type though this term covers a great variety of sub-types and this example may have been influenced by some very insular lower Severn valley types. It is fairly plain and angular, the main decoration being the groove between two bars which would have held ?enamel. Late first or second century. From Badger Hole.

No. 29 is a zoomorphic pin. The pin itself is rectangular in section and the head is modelled in the form of a horse's head with stylised decoration on the neck. Late Roman and the only object of its type from a cave. From Gough's Old Cave, Cheddar Gorge.

No. 30 is a rather crude, heavy and broken Headstud fibula. It had a cast suspension loop, hinged pin and an integrally cast stud with a ridge above. In its lack of elaboration and finesse it contrasts strongly with the following item. ?Later second century. From Culver Hole Cave, Gower.

No. 31 is probably the finest piece of bronze work from a Romano-British cave. It represents the finest type of Trumpet brooch, gilded all over and decorated in enamel, silver and ?niello. The wire suspension loop has an 'acorn' fronted clasp, the head is in the 'late Celtic' decorative style, the bow knob of finely executed petalled or acanthus type, the lower bow has devolved scrollwork in silver and the catch plate is ornately pierced. Such brooches, which mainly come from Wales, were often made in bullion metals. Their dating is disputed but is before c.150. From Lynx Cave, Clwyd. (Illustration based on that by the excavator, Mr J. D. Blore, to whom the authors are indebted for permission to use it).

No. 32 is a very small and perhaps amuletic/religious, rather than functional, plate brooch in the shape of an enamelled fish. Both this and the preceding come from probable burial caves. Second century. From Maeshafn Cave, Clwyd.

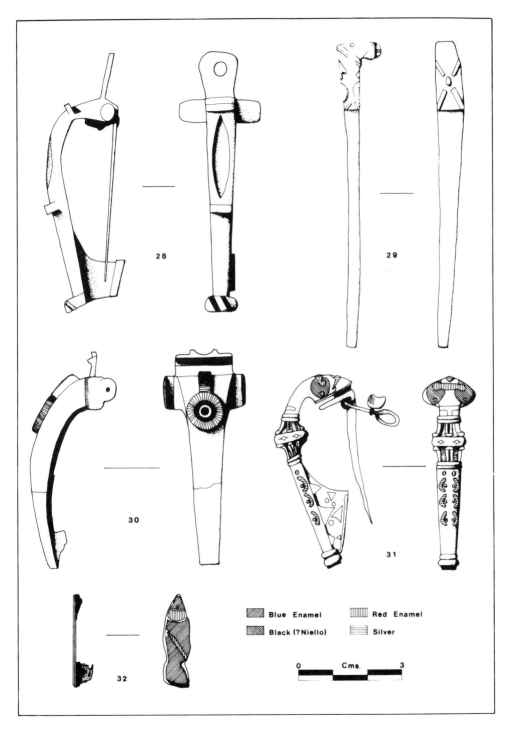

Figure A7   Bronze finds from caves in the Mendips and Wales.

An Outline Gazetteer of Romano-British Caves

A fully detailed Gazetteer of all Romano-British cave sites is available from the authors: Branigan, K. and Dearne, M.J.. A Gazetteer of Romano-British Cave Usage (Dept. of Archaeology and Prehistory, University of Sheffield, 1991), price on request. It includes details of bibliography, excavational history and all finds. Here there is only room to give a brief outline of the sites. For each site a grid reference, one or two key references (which do not necessarily cover all aspects of the site), an indication of the present location of the main finds, and brief details of the caves and their finds are given. In each case the facing page gives in tabular form a breakdown of the finds by broad category, along with some indication of the date range(s) of usage and at the bottom, code letter(s) denoting the likely form of the usage of the site.

The date ranges should be regarded as broad estimates and reflect the imprecise dating of many groups of finds. Where there are two dates one above the other, this indicates we believe there are two separate periods of usage. Where a date is preceded by "inc", it indicates specific evidence of that period (usually a coin or brooch) within material of probably much broader date range. For the finds categories question marks have been used where there is uncertainty as to whether a certain type of find was present or where there is doubt about the number of finds involved. Figures followed by a plus indicate the minimum count of objects of that class where larger numbers are believed to have been found. An X has been used where a class of finds were present but it is impossible to suggest a minimum count of items.

The usage code letters are as follows: B = burial; D = domestic; H = hideaway; O = occasional usage; R = religious; S = storage; U = unattributed; W = workshop.

Caves are prefixed according to location as follows: Caves in the Peak District and Adjacent Areas = P; Northern Britain = N; Caves in the Mendips and Southern Britain = S; Caves in Wales = W.

A number of abbreviations are used in the bibliographic references and are listed below.

Abbreviations used in Gazetteer

Arch. Camb.	Archaeologia Cambrensis
Arch. J.	Archaeological Journal
D.A.J.	Derbyshire Archaeological Journal
J.R.S.	Journal of Roman Studies
N.S.J.F.S.	North Staffordshire Journal of Field Studies
P.A.S.N.L.	Peakland Archaeological Society News Letter
P.G.P.S.W.R.Y.	Proc. of the Geological and Polytechnic Soc. of the W. Riding of Yorkshire
Proc.Soc.Ant.	Proceedings of the Society of Antiquaries
P.U.B.S.S.	Proceedings of the University of Bristol Speleological Soc.
T.C.R.G.C.B.	Trans. of the Cave Research Group of Great Britian
T.L.C.A.S.	Trans. of the Lancashire and Cheshire Archaeological Soc.
Y.A.J.	Yorkshire Archaeological Journal

P1: ASH TREE CAVE SK 5148676147

Armstrong, A.L. (1956), 'Report on the Excavation of Ash Tree Cave, Near Whitwell, Derbyshire, 1949–1957', *D.A.J.* 79, 57–64. Finds: Sheffield Museum. Platform fronted cave in dry valley site. Jars, bowls and flagon.

P2: BAT HOUSE CAVE SK 335523

Haverfield, F. (1905), 'Romano-British Remains' in *The Victoria History of the Counties of England: Derbyshire* Vol.II, 191–264. Finds: Lost. Fissure cave high in a cliff. Few details available except for Trumpet brooch.

P3: BEESTON TOR CAVE SK 106540

Wilson, G.H. (1934), *Cave Hunting Holidays in Peakland*, 47–56. Finds: Buxton Museum and Lost. Near base of Beeston Tor, Manifold Valley. Important Saxon site but poorly recorded – finds difficult to differentiate. Samian bowls and coarse jars.

P4: CHESHIRE WOOD CAVE SK 116536

Emery, G.T. (1962), 'Excavations in Falcon Low and Cheshire Wood Caves in the Manifold Valley', *N.S.J.F.S* 2, 33–6. Finds: Stoke Museum and Lost. Cliff face cave in Manifold Valley. Small amount of material, difficult to differentiate from larger amount of Iron Age occupation material.

P5: CHURN HOLE SK 16376952

Turner, M.W. (1899), *Ancient Remains Near Buxton*, 78f. Finds: Lost. Adjacent cave and rock shelter in Marl Dale. Very poorly recorded finds along with Medieval material from outside cave/shelter.

P6: UNSPECIFIED CRESWELL CRAGS CAVES c.SK 534742

See sources for P7–10. Finds: Mainly at Bolton and Manchester Museums. Finds probably from various caves in Cresswell Crags Ravine but with no exact provenances. Jars, beaker, bowl including BB ware and other miscellaneous finds. Date and usage codes not applicable.

CAVE CODE NO. ▶	P1	P2	P3	P4	P5	P6
Date Range (s)	c.200–300	c.75–150	c.75–200	?	?	?
Fine ware (Sherds)		?	3		?	1
Coarse Ware (Sherds)	10	X	11	?1	X	21
Coins						
Glass (Sherds)			1			
Fibulae		1				1
Penannular Brooches						
Ae Jewellery/ Toiletry Items						
Ae Working Evidence or Tools						
Ae Weighing Items						
Other *Ae* Finds		?1			1	
Fe Weapons						
Fe Knives						
Fe Tools						
Other *Fe* Finds				?1		1
Pb Weights						
Other *Pb* Finds						
Bone Pins/Fasteners						
Other Bone Finds			2			
Whetstones						
Other Stone Finds		1		?1		1
Skeletal Finds (No. of Individuals)						
Probable Usage	O	H	O	H	O	U

P7: CHURCH HOLE CAVE SK 53417410

Jackson, J.W. (1926), 'Recent Cave Exploration in Derbyshire', *The North West Naturalist*, 129–32 and 190–6; (1929), 'Cresswell Crags', *T.L.C.A.S.* 44, 2ff. Finds: Manchester Museum. Narrow fissure cave with few finds but including extremely fine and early Colchester derivative fibula (Figure A1 No.1).

P8: PIN HOLE CAVE SK 534742

Mello, J.M. (1875), 'Pin Hole Cave', *Quarterly Journal of the Geological Soc.* 31, 679. Finds: Manchester. Narrow fissure cave. Only find Hod Hill brooch of 43–c.65, rare this far north. (Figure A1 No.2).

P9: ROBIN'S HOOD CAVE SK 53417420

Refs. under P7 and Mello, J.M. (1875), 'On Some Bone Caves in Cresswell Crags', *Quarterly Journal of the Geological Soc.*, 679–91. Finds: Manchester and Bolton Museums. Complex set of passages. Finds mainly body sherds and Headstud brooch (Figure A1 No.3).

P10: MOTHER GRUNDY'S PARLOUR SK c.534742

Refs. under P7 and Armstrong, A.L. (1925), 'Excavations at Mother Grundy's Parlour, Cresswell Crags, Derbyshire, 1924', *Journal of the Royal Anthropological Institute* 55, 146–75. Finds: Lost. Rock shelter yielding poorly recorded pottery finds. Subsequent discoveries of brooch and coin unconfirmed.

P11: DARFUR RIDGE CAVE SK 099559

Nicholson, S. (1956), 'The Second Report on the Excavation of Darfur Ridge Cave', *P.A.S.N.L.* 21, 20–4. Finds: Lost. Small terrace fronted cave in Ecton Hill, Manifold Valley. Small number of finds from disturbed deposits.

P12: DEAD MAN'S CAVE SK 528835

White, G.F. (1970), *Excavation of Dead Man's Cave, N. Anston*. Finds: Cresswell Crags Visitors' Centre and private hands. Rectangular cave with fissure entrance in Anston Stone Gorge. A few late Roman sherds.

CAVE CODE NO. ▶	P7	P8	P9	P10	P11	P12
Date Range (s)	c.250–300	c.43–65	c.75–140	?	c.325–375	c.300–400
Fine ware (Sherds)			1	?		X
Coarse Ware (Sherds)	8		8	X	4	X
Coins				?		
Glass (Sherds)						
Fibulae	1	1	1	?1		
Penannular Brooches	1					
Ae Jewellery/ Toiletry Items			1			
Ae Working Evidence or Tools						
Ae Weighing Items						
Other *Ae* Finds						
Fe Weapons						
Fe Knives			1		1	
Fe Tools						
Other *Fe* Finds						
Pb Weights						
Other *Pb* Finds						
Bone Pins/Fasteners						
Other Bone Finds						
Whetstones						
Other Stone Finds						
Skeletal Finds (No. of Individuals)						
Probable Usage	S	S	O	S	H	O

85

P13: DOWEL CAVE SK 07556760

Bramwell, D. (1959), 'Excavation of Dowel Cave, Earl Sterndale 1958–9', *D.A.J.* 79, 97–109. Finds: ?Lost. Fissure cave only yielding a few finds whose dates have not been verified.

P14: ELDERBUSH CAVE SK 098549

Bramwell, D. (1964), 'The Excavations at Elder Bush Cave, Wetton, Staffs', *N.S.J.F.S.* 4, 46–60. Finds: Buxton Museum. Largely choked cave fronted by tallus, both yielding much pottery, notably Derbyshire ware jars, and other finds including unusual Trumpet brooch (Figure A2 No.4).

P15: FISSURE CAVE SK 16518030

Pill, A.L. (1963), 'Some Recent Discoveries in the Hartle Dale Caves', *Proc. of the British Speleological Association* 1, 5–13. Finds: In private hands. Cave fronted by a rock fissure. Limited details of finds include jar(s).

P16: FOX HOLE CAVE SK 100663

Bramwell, D. (1971), 'Report on the Excavations at Fox Hole Cave, High Weeldon 1961–1970', *D.A.J.* 91, 1–19. Finds: Buxton Museum and Lost. Finds from entrance/first chamber of long irregular tunnel-like system near summit of High Weeldon Hill. Pottery mainly samian. Skeletal finds and bronze armlet (Figure A2 No.5).

P17: FRANK-I-TH-ROCKS CAVE SK 13125843

Palmer, L.S. and Lee, L.S. (1925), 'Frank-i-th-Rocks Cave and Other Northern Caves in Relation to the Ice Ages', *P.U.B.S.S.* 2iii, 244–60. Finds: Buxton Museum and Lost. Narrow, twisting tunnel cave. Finds inc. jars, bowls, olla, glass beads, coins, bronze work (inc. Figure A2 No.6), skeletal remains etc.

P18: HARBOROUGH CAVE SK 24225522

Storrs-Fox, W. (1909), 'Harborough Cave near Brassington', *D.A.J.* 31, 89–114; Armstrong, A.L. (1923), 'Exploration of Harborough Cave, Brassington', *Journal of the Royal Anthropological Institute* 53, 402–16. Finds: British and Sheffield Museums and Lost. Large cave in Harborough Rocks. Poorly recorded. Probably far more material recovered than can be listed, pottery in particular. Finds inc. Fe spears and Pb weight (Figure A2 No.7).

CAVE CODE NO. ▶	P13	P14	P15	P16	P17	P18
Date Range (s)	?	c.60–300	c.260–400	c.75–200	c.100–200 c.325–375	c.75–150/200
Fine ware (Sherds)		4	X	15	2	?1
Coarse Ware (Sherds)	?2	74	X	2+	23+	3+
Coins			3		10	3
Glass (Sherds)					8	
Fibulae		1			1	3
Penannular Brooches					1	1
Ae Jewellery/ Toiletry Items		1		1	1+	
Ae Working Evidence or Tools						
Ae Weighing Items						
Other *Ae* Finds		1			5	
Fe Weapons						3
Fe Knives		1				2
Fe Tools		?1				
Other *Fe* Finds		4+			5+	11
Pb Weights						1
Other *Pb* Finds			1			
Bone Pins/Fasteners		1			1	
Other Bone Finds	1	1	1+		7	
Whetstones		2			1	1
Other Stone Finds		7			2	8
Skeletal Finds (No. of Individuals)				?1	10+	
Probable Usage	H	D	O	B	B/O	D

P19: NO NAME KNOWN SK 14676630

J.R.S. 18 (1928), 198–9. Finds: Lost. Small coin hoard in obscure cave.

P20: OLD WOMAN'S HOUSE CAVE SK 16537085

Storrs-Fox, W. (1911), 'Derbyshire Cave-Men of the Roman Period', *D.A.J.* 33, 115–26. Finds: Buxton Museum and Lost. Small, high cave in Taddington Dale Cliffs with a very small creep entrance. Finds included little pottery but bronze brooches (inc. Figure A2 No.8 and Figure A3 No.9) and iron work.

P21: OSSUMS CRAG CAVE SK 095557

Bramwell, D. (1954, 5 and 6) Reports in *P.A.S.N.L.* 11, 12 and 13. Finds: Stoke Museum. Small fissure cave below P22. Only finds Derbyshire Ware, BB jars and whetstones.

P22: OSSUMS EYRIE CAVE SK 095557

Bramwell, D. (1956, 7 and 8) Reports in *P.A.S.N.L.* 13, 14 and 15. Finds: Manchester Museum. Small inaccessible ledge-fronted cave above P21. Small group of finds, most notably brooch (Figure A3 No.10) and knife (Figure A3 No.11).

P23: POOLE'S CAVERN SK 05007251

Bramwell, D. et al (1983), 'Excavations at Poole's Cavern, Buxton: An Interim Report', *D.A.J.* 103, 47–74; Branigan, K. and Bayley, J. (1989), 'The Romano-British Metalwork from Poole's Cavern, Buxton', *D.A.J.* 109, 34–50. Finds: Buxton and site Museums. Large and important cave near Buxton. Very large finds assemblage including very varied pottery. Most important elements – much bronze working waste and tools, wide array of brooches and decorative bronze work (some unfinished) and unique lead mould formers for brooches and accessories. Also burials. Iron finds may be heavily underestimated due to identification problems, as may glass. Further material probably lost without record.

P24: PYMM'S PARLOUR SK 00319443

Hamnett, R. (1899), 'Melandra Castle, Derbyshire', *D.A.J.* 31, 10–19. Finds: Lost. Small and obscure 'cave' near Melandra Roman fort apparently yielding an uncertain number of coins and bronze plate (date in doubt).

CAVE CODE NO. ▶	P19	P20	P21	P22	P23	P24
Date Range (s)	c.325	c.80–150 c.310	c.150–250	c.125–225	c.80–225	c.275–350
Fine ware (Sherds)					26+	
Coarse Ware (Sherds)		6	10	1	637+	
Coins	9+	2+			19+	4+
Glass (Sherds)				1	2(?+)	
Fibulae		2		1	29 or 30	
Penannular Brooches		2			13	
Ae Jewellery/ Toiletry Items					24	
Ae Working Evidence or Tools					42	
Ae Weighing Items						
Other *Ae* Finds				2	100	1
Fe Weapons						
Fe Knives		2		1	1	
Fe Tools		?1				
Other *Fe* Finds		10			3	
Pb Weights					1	
Other *Pb* Finds					41	
Bone Pins/Fasteners		1		1	1	
Other Bone Finds		5			11	
Whetstones		2	3			
Other Stone Finds		5		1	4	
Skeletal Finds (No. of Individuals)					6+	
Probable Usage	H	H	H	H	W,D,B	H

P25: RAVENCLIFFE CAVE SK 17407357

Simth, R.A. (1912), 'Ravencliffe Cave', *D.A.J.* 32, 141–57; Storrs-Fox, W. (1928), 'Ravencliffe Cave', *D.A.J.* 50, 71–8. Finds: British and Buxton Museums. Large irregular cave reached from cliff top. Most notable finds fibula and penannular brooch (Figure A3 Nos.12 and 13).

P26: REYNARD'S CAVE SK 14505252

Kelly, J.H. (1960), 'Excavations at Reynard's Cave, Dovedale 1959', *D.A.J.* 80, 117–23. Finds: Buxton Museum. Large cave in cliff face above R. Dove. Colour Coated wares, coarse ware jars, bowls, flagons and mortarium, unsubstantiated coin hoard and brooch (Figure A4 No.14). Not fully excavated.

P27: SEVEN WAYS CAVE SK 098549

Bramwell, D. (1952 and 1954) Reports in *P.A.S.N.L.* 8 and 10. Finds: Lost and in private hands. Burial ?associated with glass bead and undateable items. Dating generally problematic.

P28: THIRST HOUSE CAVE SK 09717129

Branigan, K. and Dearne, M.J. (forthcoming), 'The Small Finds from Thirst House Cave, Deepdale: A Reappraisal' in Smith, K. and Hodges, R., *Recent Developments in the Archaeology of the Peak District*. Finds: Buxton Museum and Lost. Large cave with tallus in Deepdale, near Buxton. Finds including many varied brooches and other decorative metalwork, notably a very fine Trumpet brooch and toiletry set. Series of rings at various stages of manufacture. Burials outside cave. Much material lost without record.

P29: THOR'S CAVE SK 098549

Brown, M.E. (1964), 'Report on the Exploration of Thor's Cave', *Trans. Midland Scientific Association*, 1–6, 19–20, 70–1. Finds: Derby Museum and Lost. Large, prominent cave with several occupation layers. Very poorly recorded and originally far more finds, especially pottery. Brooches (Figure A4 Nos.15–17 and Figure A5 No.18) and ironwork notable.

P30: THOR'S FISSURE CAVE SK 099550

Wilson, G.H. (1934), 'Cave Hunting Holidays in Peakland', 13–46. Finds: Buxton Museum. Fissure cave near P29. Bowls, ?jars and flagon; earring; iron brooch (Figure A5 No.19).

CAVE CODE NO. ▶	P25	P26	P27	P28	P29	P30
Date Range (s)	c.75–125	c.150–400	c.50/100	c.100–200 c.250–275	c.75–225	c.75–175
Fine ware (Sherds)	4	5		1+	?	1
Coarse Ware (Sherds)	2	80	2+	81+	X	16
Coins		X		9	1	
Glass (Sherds)	6		1	3	1	
Fibulae	1	1		23	5	1
Penannular Brooches				17		
Ae Jewellery/ Toiletry Items			1	17	2+	1
Ae Working Evidence or Tools				8		
Ae Weighing Items						
Other Ae Finds		3	1	23		1+
Fe Weapons				1	1+	
Fe Knives				3	3+	
Fe Tools				3	2	
Other Fe Finds	2	8	1	68+	16	1+
Pb Weights						
Other Pb Finds		2		6	1	
Bone Pins/Fasteners				7	1	1
Other Bone Finds		4		8	3	4
Whetstones	2			3	2+	1
Other Stone Finds	2			10	4	
Skeletal Finds (No. of Individuals)			1	?4		?6+
Probable Usage	O	H	O	W,D,B	D	H

P31: UPPER CALES DALE CAVE SK 17306541

Derbyshire S.M.R. Finds: Lost. Higher of two caves in Lathkill Dale. Little known and sometimes confused with other sites. Only 'RB' sherds recorded.

P32: WETTON MILL ROCK SHELTER SK 096563

Kelly, J.H. (1976), *The Excavation of Wetton Mill Rock Shelter, Manifold Valley, Staffs.* Finds: Stoke Museum. Small rock shelter. Finds mainly sherds of beaker, jars and bowls.

N1: ATTERMIRE CAVE SD 842642

King, A. (1970), 'Romano-British Metalwork from the Settle District of West Yorkshire', *Y.A.J.* 62, 410–17. Finds: mainly in private hands. Narrow passages and chambers in cliff above drained mire nr. Settle. Few details available except for brooches (inc. one in silver) and a few other finds. Many more finds suspected.

N2: BRIDES CHAIR CAVE SD 481731

Harrison, P.A. (1974), 'The Caves of North West Lancashire and South Cumbria', *Contrebis* 2ii, 34–5. Finds: Lancaster Museum. Obscure cave apparently with jar sherds.

N3: DOG HOLES CAVE (Warton Crag) SD 48337303

Jackson, J.W. (1912), 'Report on the Recent Explorations at Dog Holes, Warton Crag', *T.C.W.A.A.S.* 12, 55–8. Finds: Lancaster Museum. Multi-chambered cave below limestone pavement. Incompletely recorded pottery group; diverse bronze finds including balance (Figure A5 No.20), binding (Figure A5 No.21) and fastener (Figure A5 No.22); ironwork inc. pruning hook; ?RB skeletal material. Also possible evidence of iron smelting.

N4: DOG HOLES CAVE (Haverbrack Bank) SD 803484

Benson, D. and Bland, K. (1963), 'The Dog Hole, Haverbrack', *T.C.W.A.A.S.* 63, 61–76. Finds: Lancaster Museum. Passage cave below limestone pavement. Much skeletal material, along with bracelets, finger rings, jet beads, axe head etc.

CAVE CODE NO.	P31	P32	N1	N2	N3	N4
Date Range (s)	?	c.175–225 c.275	c.?55–200 c.250–350	?	c.90–125 c.175–225	c.300–400
Fine ware (Sherds)		2	?		1 (?+)	
Coarse Ware (Sherds)	X	5	X	7	6+	
Coins		1	4			
Glass (Sherds)						
Fibulae			15		1	
Penannular Brooches			13			1
Ae Jewellery/Toiletry Items			X		2	8
Ae Working Evidence or Tools					1	
Ae Weighing Items					1	
Other *Ae* Finds					1 or 2	
Fe Weapons			1			
Fe Knives			1		2	
Fe Tools			?2+			1
Other *Fe* Finds			2	1	28	X
Pb Weights						
Other *Pb* Finds				2	1	
Bone Pins/Fasteners						
Other Bone Finds				3		
Whetstones					1	3
Other Stone Finds			1		1	10
Skeletal Finds (No. of Individuals)					?X	23+
Probable Usage	O	O	D	H	B,H	B

N5: DOWKERBOTTOM HOLE SD 952689

Farrer, J.W. (1857), 'Dowkerbottom Hole', *Proc.Soc.Ant.* 4, 111–2; Farrer, J. and Denny, H. (1866), 'Further Exploration in the Dowkerbottom Caves, in Craven', *P.G.P.S.W.R.Y.* 4, 45–74; Poulton, E.B. (1881), 'A Preliminary Account of the Working of Dowkerbottom Cave...1881', *P.G.P.S.W.R.Y.* 7, 351–68. Finds: British Museum and very many Lost. Large cave below limestone pavement with shaft entrance. Recorded finds include numbers of brooches (inc. Figure A6 No.23) and other decorated bronze work (inc. Figure A6 Nos.24–5); coins; large bone assemblage including decorated 'spoon brooches'. Much pottery and probably other finds are lost without record.

N6: FAIRY HOLE SD 49687294

Jackson, J.W. (1910), 'Further Report on the Exploration at Dog Holes, Warton Crag, Lancs. with Remarks on the Contents of Two Adjacent Caves', *T.L.C.A.S.* 28, 61–82. Finds: Lancaster Museum. Small fissure cave. Few finds.

N7: JUBILEE CAVE SD 838656

Raistrick, A. (1939), 'Iron Age Settlements in West Yorkshire', *Y.A.J.* 34, 115–50. Finds: in private hands. Series of passages/chambers in cliff nr. Settle. Poorly known assemblage including jars, a few metal, bone and stone items. It is not known how much material was found or is extant.

N8: GREATER KELCO CAVE SD 810646

Disparate sources inc. refs. under N1 and N7. Finds: Lost and in private hands. Large rock shelter in Giggleswick Scar. Small varied assemblage with little pottery but five coins and several brooches including Dragonesques.

N9: LESSER KELCO CAVE SD 810646

Source as ref. under N7. Finds: in private hands. Small rock shelter adjacent to N8. Very poorly known small assemblage.

N10: KING ALFRID'S CAVE SE 898833

Lamplough, W.H. and Lidster, J.R. (1959), 'The Excavation of King Alfrid's Cave, Ebberston' *Trans. Scarborough and District Arch. Soc.* 1ii,16–31. Finds: Scarborough Museum. Small cave yielding four coarse sherds.

CAVE CODE NO. ▶	N5	N6	N7	N8	N9	N10
Date Range (s)	c.55–375	c.50–100	? (inc. c.310)	c.75–150 c.250–300	?	c.325–75
Fine ware (Sherds)	X	5	1	1	?	
Coarse Ware (Sherds)	X	2	10+	3	X	4
Coins	?10		1	5+		
Glass (Sherds)	4					
Fibulae	6 or 7 (?+)			5		
Penannular Brooches	3		2+	4	1+	
Ae Jewellery/ Toiletry Items	9+					
Ae Working Evidence or Tools						
Ae Weighing Items						
Other *Ae* Finds	27+			1		
Fe Weapons	1		?2			
Fe Knives	2					
Fe Tools						
Other *Fe* Finds	6+	1	1	3		
Pb Weights						
Other *Pb* Finds	2		2+	1		
Bone Pins/Fasteners	3		2+	3+	1+	
Other Bone Finds	27		4	2	1+	
Whetstones	1		1			
Other Stone Finds	7+	1	3+	2	1 (?+)	
Skeletal Finds (No. of Individuals)			?			
Probable Usage	D	B	D	O	D	O

N11: KINSEY CAVE SD 804657

Jackson, J.W. and Mattinson, W.K. (1932), 'A Cave on Giggleswick Scars, nr.Settle, Yorkshire', *The Naturalist* January, 5–9. Finds: in private hands. Large rock shelter. Unspecified amounts of pottery and limited number of other items but notably including toilet spoon and lorica segmentata buckle.

N12: KIRKHEAD CAVE SD 39107565

Morris, J.P. (1866), 'Report of Explorations Conducted in the Kirkhead Cave at Ulverstone', *Memoirs of the Anthropological Society of London* 2, 358–63. Finds: Lost. Large shore line cave. Small number of finds, only the coin certainly Roman.

N13: UNNAMED CAVE AT LEYBURN SHAWL SE c.1190

Ref. as N7. Finds: ?Lost. Small obscure cave with poorly known finds.

N14: MERLEWOOD CAVE SD c.3975

Ref. as N2. Finds: ?Lost. Obscure cave with poorly recorded finds.

N15: SEWELL'S CAVE SD 786666

Raistrick, A. (1936), 'Excavations at Sewell's Cave, Settle, W. Yorkshire', *Proc. of the University of Durham Philosophical Soc.* 9, 191–204. Finds: in private hands. Large but shallow cave in Common Scar, Settle. The only reasonably published cave in the Settle area, but even so only a small selection of the pottery is known in detail (bowls, mortaria and jars). Bronze finds included mainly brooches and bone work included a comb and 'spoon brooches'. Most important finds are in iron, including knives, a key, vessel fragments, a projectile head and two sword blades (perhaps semispatha).

N16: SPIDER CAVE SD 824640

Ref. as for N1. Finds: in private hands. Obscure ?small cave yielding only a first century broken bronze mirror handle.

CAVE CODE NO. ▶	N11	N12	N13	N14	N15	N16
Date Range (s)	c.100–250	c.80–100	?	?	c.75–275	c.50–100
Fine ware (Sherds)	2		X	X	1+	
Coarse Ware (Sherds)	X		X		11+	
Coins		1			1	
Glass (Sherds)						
Fibulae	1				5	
Penannular Brooches	1 (?+)				3	
Ae **Jewellery/ Toiletry Items**		1				1
Ae **Working Evidence or Tools**						
Ae **Weighing Items**						
Other *Ae* **Finds**	4	5			7	
Fe **Weapons**					3	
Fe **Knives**		1			4	
Fe **Tools**		1 or 2				
Other *Fe* **Finds**	1				5	
Pb **Weights**						
Other *Pb* **Finds**	1				1	
Bone Pins/Fasteners	2				2	
Other Bone Finds	4		X		11	
Whetstones			X			
Other Stone Finds	2+		X		4	
Skeletal Finds (No. of Individuals)				?X		
Probable Usage	O	O	D	U	D	U

N17: TOM TAYLOR'S CHAMBER SE c0974

Speight, H. (1906), *Nidderdale*. Finds: Lost. Little known cave in How Stean Gorge. Finds two or more coins.

N18: VICTORIA AND ALBERT CAVES SD 838650

Very disparate sources inc. Dawkins, W.B. (1874), *Cave Hunting*; Smith, C.R. (1844) *Collectanea Antiqua* II, 69–72; Tiddeman R.H. (1875), 'The Works and Problems of the Victoria Cave Exploration', *P.G.P.S.W.R.Y.* 6, 77ff. The only unified account is in the full version of this gazetteer. Finds: British and Buxton Museums, in private hands and probably Lost. Two adjacent series of passages and chambers in Kings Scar nr. Settle. Very large and important collection of finds with possible very great quantities of material lost without record or unpublished in private hands. Very important group of bronze brooches, notably S-shaped and Dragonesques probably reflecting manufacturing activity. Also other decorative bronze work. Known pottery (probably a fraction of the assemblage) including fineware, and coarse jars and bowls; glass vessels and armlets; at least 31 coins but sources hard to reconcile; iron and stone finds probably very under-represented in sources; large bone assemblage including 'spoon brooches'. Only systematic assessment is in full gazetteer but many questions remain.

N19: UNCERTAIN CAVES IN THE SETTLE AREA

Six objects from uncertain caves (perhaps N5 or N18) in British Museum including brooch (Figure A6 No.27).

S1: ANSTEY'S CAVE SX 936647

Ref. as under P2. Finds: Lost. Small sea cliff with very badly recorded finds.

S2: ASH HOLE SX c.9456

Ref. as S1. Finds: Lost. Coastal cave with very badly recorded finds.

S3: BACKWELL CAVE ST 49246801

Tratman, E.K. and Jackson, J.W. (1938), 'The Excavation of Backwell Cave, Somerset', *P.U.B.S.S.* 5i, 57–74. Finds: Destroyed. Small Mendip cave. Apparently used as a burial site 100 B.C. – A.D.100.

CAVE CODE NO. ▶	N17	N18	N19	S1	S2	S3
Date Range (s)	inc. c.55–70	c.50–400	?	inc. c.140–160	c.55–70	c.50–100
Fine ware (Sherds)		X			?	
Coarse Ware (Sherds)		13+		?	X	2+
Coins	2+	?31		2	1	
Glass (Sherds)		20				
Fibulae		36 or 37	1			
Penannular Brooches		5				
Ae Jewellery/ Toiletry Items		17+				
Ae Working Evidence or Tools						
Ae Weighing Items		?1				
Other *Ae* Finds		25+		1		
Fe Weapons		1+				
Fe Knives		3				
Fe Tools		1				
Other *Fe* Finds		15+				
Pb Weights						
Other *Pb* Finds			1			
Bone Pins/Fasteners		14				
Other Bone Finds		38+	4			
Whetstones		1+				
Other Stone Finds		15+				1
Skeletal Finds (No. of Individuals)					?	18+
Probable Usage	U	W,D	U	H	O	B

S4: BADGER HOLE ST 53244795

Balch, H.E. (1947), 'The Great Cave of Wookey Hole' in *The Mendip Caves*, 78–83. Finds: Wells Museum. Large chambered cave. Finds include a brooch (Plate 7 No.28); fine ware, coarse jars, bowls and dishes; a coin; and a badly corroded, perhaps modern group of iron work.

S5: BROWNE'S HOLE ST 66934757

Unpublished. Finds: Frome Museum. Large entrance passage with small chambers. Flagon, bowl and jar sherds, some imitating samian forms, and two coins.

S6: CALLOW LIMEWATER CAVE ST 44785575

Smith, D.I. (1975), *Limestones and Caves of the Mendip Hills*, 384. Finds: Lost. Small cave nr.Shipham with badly recorded coin finds.

S7: CHARTERHOUSE WARREN FARM SWALLET ST 49365458

Levitan, B.M. et al (1973), 'Charterhouse Warren Farm Swallet, Mendip, Somerset. Exploration, Geomorphology, Taphonomy, and Archaeology', *P.U.B.S.S.* 18ii, 171–239. Finds: Wells Museum and ?Lost. Vertical burial shaft used from Neolithic to Romano-British times. One certain RB burial in side passage with a little pottery, Ae ring, shale armlet etc.

S8: GOUGH'S OLD CAVE ST 46685388

Branigan, K. and Dearne, M.J. (forthcoming), 'Romano-British Usage of the Caves of Cheddar Gorge', *P.U.B.S.S.* Finds: Cheddar Caves and U.B.S.S. Museums and very much Lost. Large tunnel-like cave extended as show cave in Cheddar Gorge. Only a small amount of material extant of a probably very large but little recorded assemblage removed in nineteenth century. Pottery and bronze work likely to have been important. Notable zoomorphic pin (Figure A7 No.29).

S9: GOUGH'S NEW CAVE ST 46685388

Ref. as under S8. Finds: Cheddar Caves and Weston Super Mare Museums and much probably Lost. Similar to and below S8 but more choked in Romano-British times. Very poorly recorded finds and much probably lost without record.

CAVE CODE NO. ➤	S4	S5	S6	S7	S8	S9
Date Range (s)	c.75–160 c.225–275	c.150–200 c.275–325	?	c.50–100	c.300–400	c.300–400
Fine ware (Sherds)	4			1	1	?
Coarse Ware (Sherds)	212	13		4	23	45+
Coins	1	2	X		1	4
Glass (Sherds)						1
Fibulae	1					
Penannular Brooches						
Ae Jewellery/ Toiletry Items					2	
Ae Working Evidence or Tools						
Ae Weighing Items						
Other *Ae* Finds				1	2	
Fe Weapons						
Fe Knives						
Fe Tools						
Other *Fe* Finds	?40			1		
Pb Weights						
Other *Pb* Finds						
Bone Pins/Fasteners						
Other Bone Finds					3	
Whetstones	1					3
Other Stone Finds				1		9
Skeletal Finds (No. of Individuals)				1		
Probable Usage	O	O	U	B	D	D

S10: LONG HOLE (AND THE SLITTER) ST 46685387

Ref. as under S8. Finds: Cheddar Caves Museum and much probably Lost. Large, important cave adjacent to, but higher than, S8 and S9 with a large dump of material (the Slitter) below it. Very much material lost, often without records. Extant material includes many colour coated vessels, notably a flagon with cast female head, two steelyard arms and much other decorative bronzework and ?scrap. Large number of coins (Boon, G.C. (1957), 'Roman Coins from Gough's Old cave and the Slitter, Cheddar', *Numismatic Chronicle*, 6th s.17, 231–7; the provenance corrected in Branigan and Dearne).

S11: PRIDE EVANS' HOLE ST 46815406

Ref. as under S8. Finds: Lost. Small cave near the base of Cheddar Gorge. Only finds a coin hoard, badly recorded and of dubious authenticity.

S12: SOLDIER'S HOLE ST 46875400

Ref. as under S8. Finds: *U.B.S.S.* Museum and Lost. Large but very difficult of access. Small group of finds including one jar and a coin.

S13: SUN HOLE ST 46735408

Ref. as under S8. Finds: *U.B.S.S.* and Lost. Large but very difficult of access. Up to eight vessels, three coins and a fragment of a fourth and a shale bracelet.

S14: CHELM'S COMBE ROCK SHELTER ST 46345447

Balch, H.E. and Palmer (1926), 'Excavations at Chelm's Combe, Cheddar', *P.S.A.N.H.S.* 72, 93–124. Finds: Lost. Small cliff overhung shelter near Cheddar Gorge. Finds included a few sherds of pottery, four coins and an Aucissa brooch of the mid-first century before c.80.

S15: DINDER WOOD SHELTER ST 58844541

Balch, H.E. (1937), *Mendip – Its Swallet Caves and Rock Shelters*. Finds: Wells Museum and Lost. Cave in Dinder Ravine. Finds only a small group of pottery predominant in jars.

CAVE CODE NO. ▶	S10	S11	S12	S13	S14	S15
Date Range (s)	c.250–400	c.270–275	c.250–300	c.275–350	c.50–80 c.310–50	c.200–300
Fine ware (Sherds)	40+					c.60
Coarse Ware (Sherds)	24+		3+	8	4+	
Coins	375 (+)	47	1	4	4	
Glass (Sherds)	1					
Fibulae					1	
Penannular Brooches	1					
Ae Jewellery/ Toiletry Items	20		1			
Ae Working Evidence or Tools	?13					
Ae Weighing Items	2					
Other *Ae* Finds	27					
Fe Weapons	4					
Fe Knives						
Fe Tools						
Other *Fe* Finds	8					
Pb Weights						
Other *Pb* Finds	3					
Bone Pins/Fasteners						
Other Bone Finds		4				
Whetstones						
Other Stone Finds	1			1		
Skeletal Finds (No. of Individuals)						
Probable Usage	D	H	H	H	O	O

S16: HEY WOOD CAVE ST 33995822

Everton, A. and Everton, R. (1972), 'Hey Wood Cave Burials, Mendip Hills, Somerset', *P.U.B.S.S.* 13i, 5–29. Finds: Axbridge Museum. Small cave in steep hillside. Small group of pottery in disturbed mound also containing many skeletal remains, some of which might be Romano-British.

S17: KENT'S CAVERN SX 93456415

Silvester, R.J. (1986), 'The Later Prehistoric and Roman Material from Kent's Cavern, Torquay', *Devon Archaeological Society Proc.* 44, 9–38. Two adjacent entrances to two sets of chambers and passages. Majority of finds pre-Roman but sherds of fine ware, amphorae and coarse pots and bowls; two coins; spoon.

S18: LITTLE CAVE, EBBOR ST 52464862

Balch, H.E. (1913, 1919, 1922), Reports in *Mendip Nature Research Council Report* 6, 12 and 15. Finds: Wells Museum. Small cave high in Ebbor Gorge. Finds only four small body sherds.

S19: ROWBERROW CAVERN ST 45965802

Taylor, H. (1921–5), Reports in *P.U.B.S.S.* 1ii, 1iii, 2i, 2ii and 2iii. Finds: Destroyed. Rectangular cave with large entrance near Rowberrow village, Mendips. Poor publications make assessing finds difficult and site important in the Iron Age. Few details available of pottery but a considerable number of coin finds and perhaps counterfeiting evidence.

S20: SCRAGG'S HOLE ST 398559

Ref. as under S15. Finds: Lost. Short, roomy cave near Compton Bishop. Very few details of finds available but pottery, glass and a coin of Magnentius seem to have been included.

S21: TAYLORS WOOD CAVE ST 44836438

Richards, C. (forthcoming), 'The Cave' in Rahtz, P. and Watts, L., *Excavations at Cadbury, Congresbury*. Finds: Lost. Small cave c.140m from Roman Villa. Only finds skeletal (RB attribution rests on proximity to villa).

CAVE CODE NO.	S16	S17	S18	S19	S20	S21
Date Range (s)	c.150–250 c.350–400	c.50–75 post 270	?	inc 275–300	inc c.350	?
Fine ware (Sherds)	4	1		?		
Coarse Ware (Sherds)	88	44	4	c.20 vessels	X	
Coins		2		23	1	
Glass (Sherds)					X	
Fibulae						
Penannular Brooches						
Ae **Jewellery/ Toiletry Items**						
Ae **Working Evidence or Tools**						
Ae **Weighing Items**						
Other *Ae* Finds		1		5+		
Fe **Weapons**						
Fe **Knives**						
Fe **Tools**						
Other *Fe* Finds						
Pb **Weights**						
Other *Pb* Finds				1		
Bone Pins/Fasteners						
Other Bone Finds						
Whetstones						
Other Stone Finds						
Skeletal Finds (No. of Individuals)	?					4
Probable Usage	B	O	H	H	O	B

S22: TICKENHAM ROCK SHELTER ST 44417218

Savory, J.H. (1924), 'The Tickenham Rock Shelter', *P.U.B.S.S.* 2ii, 173–5. Finds: Taunton Museum and Clevedon Arch.Soc. Small rock shelter. Mainly an imperfectly known small pottery assemblage.

S23 TOM TIVY'S HOLE ST 70514447

Barrett, J.H. (1965), 'Tom Tivy's Hole Rock Shelter, near Leighton, Somerset', *P.U.B.S.S.* 11i, 9–24. Finds: Bristol Museum and Lost. Small rock shelter with a small assemblage of pottery.

S24: UPHILL (QUARRY) CAVES NOS.2 & 10 ST 31595836

Harrison, R.A. (1977), 'Uphill Quarry Caves, Weston-super-Mare: A Reappraisal', *P.U.B.S.S.* 14iii, 233–54. Finds: Lost. Cliff base cave now destroyed. Badly recorded coin ?hoard in Cave 2 (Ag and Ae mainly Valentinian and Gratian, perhaps c.200 coins) and pottery sherds. Cave 10 contains a few sherds and stone artifacts.

S25: WHITE WOMANS HOLE ST 70334433

Barret, J.H. and Boon, G.C. (1972), 'A Roman Counterfeiter's Den', *P.U.B.S.S.* 13i, 61–82. Finds: Bristol City and U.B.S.S. Museum. Fairly well hidden tunnel cave with extensive counterfeiting evidence and two later coin finds.

S26: WOOKEY HOLE ST 532479

Branigan, K. and Dearne, M.J. (forthcoming), 'The Romano-British Finds from Wookey Hole: A Reappraisal', *P.U.B.S.S.* Finds: Wells and Site Museums. A very important and large cave system. Probably at first used for ?burials and later as occupation/?workshop area with cemetery in fourth chamber. Very extensive finds, some not listed opposite because of dating problems (cf. Appendix to Branigan and Dearne). Quantities of fineware and of coarse mortaria, dishes, bowls, beakers, jars, flagons. Large number of coins inc. ?hoard. Several brooches and various other bronze work. Probably more iron work than listed. Lead or lead/tin bars. Important collection of bone pins. Many finished and unfinished stone spindle whorls.

W1: BACON HOLE SS 56058683

Allen, E.E. and Rutter, J.G. (1946), *A Survey of the Gower Caves with an Account of Recent Excavations*. Finds: Lost. Large coastal cave in Gower Peninsula. Coarse sherd and two bone finds.

CAVE CODE NO. ▶	S22	S23	S24	S25	S26	W1
Date Range (s)	c.200–400	inc c.275–325	c.380–400	c.280/300 & c.350–400	inc c.125–75 c.250–400	c.100–200
Fine ware (Sherds)		?1			122	
Coarse Ware (Sherds)	44+	?4	X	4	2743	1
Coins			129+	441	134	
Glass (Sherds)					4	
Fibulae					10	
Penannular Brooches				1	6	
***Ae* Jewellery/ Toiletry Items**					26	
***Ae* Working Evidence or Tools**						
***Ae* Weighing Items**						
Other *Ae* Finds	1				6+	
***Fe* Weapons**						
***Fe* Knives**						
***Fe* Tools**					3	
Other *Fe* Finds				1	46	
***Pb* Weights**						
Other *Pb* Finds					13	
Bone Pins/Fasteners					43+	1
Other Bone Finds					1	1+
Whetstones					24+	
Other Stone Finds			2+	1	21+	
Skeletal Finds (No. of Individuals)					47+	
Probable Usage	O	O	H	H	B,W,D	O

W2: B.S. POTHOLE SJ 0071

Valdemar, A.E. and Jones, R.D. (1970), 'An Initial Report on the Archaeological and Palaeontological Caves and Rock Shelters in North Wales', *T.C.R.G.C.B.* 12ii, 99–107. Finds: ?Shrops. Mining Club. Very few details of finds or cave.

W3: CULVER HOLE SS 40589296

Ref. as under W1 but (1948) Part 2. Finds: National Museum of Wales, Ashmolean Museum and Lost. Large chamber with slit-like entrance on coast of Gower Peninsula. Many of finds badly recorded but several coins and other finds inc. a small bronze ?mother goddess figurine from a ?votive deposit near the entrance. No details of pottery finds available and some finds may be lost without record but extant material incudes brooch (Plate 7 No.30).

W4: GREAT ORME'S HEAD CAVE SH 78008284

Jackson, J.W. (1962), 'Archaeology and Palaeontology', in Cullingford, C.H.D., *British Caving*, 291ff. Finds: Lost. Small sea cave in Great Orme's Head. Coin only noted by Jackson.

W5: KING ARTHUR'S CAVE SO c.5515

Hewer, T.F. (1928), 'King Arthur's Cave, near Whitchurch, Ross-on-Wye', *P.U.B.S.S.* 3ii, 59–83. Finds: Almost all Lost. Two passages leading off of large entrance in Wye Valley. Few details of a probably small pottery assemblage.

W6: LESSER GARTH CAVE ST 126822

Hussey, M.S. (1966), 'Final Excavations at the Lesser Garth Cave, Pentyrch', *Transactions of the Cardiff Naturalists Soc.* 93, 18–39. Finds: National Museum of Wales. Tunnel-like cave at top of a steep slope. Finds from hearths near entrance and ?rubbish dump. Mainly coarse jars and stone finds.

W7: LITTLE HOYLE SN 112001

Rolleston et al (1878), *Trans. Br. Association*, 209–17. Finds: Tenby and National Museum of Wales and ?Lost. Two chambered cave. Finds badly recorded. Amount of material recoverd and date of much in doubt. Many Dark Age finds?

CAVE CODE NO. ▸	W2	W3	W4	W5	W6	W7
Date Range (s)	c.200–400	c.100–200 inc c.300–350	inc 80–90	inc 200–300	c.250–300 or c.180–400	?
Fine ware (Sherds)	?			?		1
Coarse Ware (Sherds)	X	?		X	85	7+
Coins		16+	1			?1
Glass (Sherds)		1				
Fibulae		2+				
Penannular Brooches		1				
Ae Jewellery/ Toiletry Items		1				
Ae Working Evidence or Tools						
Ae Weighing Items						
Other *Ae* Finds		1				
Fe Weapons						
Fe Knives						
Fe Tools		?1				
Other *Fe* Finds		1				1+
Pb Weights						
Other *Pb* Finds						
Bone Pins/Fasteners						
Other Bone Finds						
Whetstones					?7	
Other Stone Finds		1			?1	
Skeletal Finds (No. of Individuals)						
Probable Usage	O	R	U	O	O	O

W8 LLANYMYNECH SJ 265223

Unpublished. Finds; In private hands. No information on cave. Only find a Trumpet brooch – no details.

W9: LYNX CAVE SJ 194593

Blore, J.D. (1981) 1962–1981 *Lynx Cave Excavations*, Clwyd. Finds: In private hands. Very small fissure cave c.1 mile from W10. Only RB finds two armlet frags, and extremely fine brooch (Figure A7 No.31), ?and skeletal remains.

W10: MAESHAFN CAVE SJ 198605

Hesketh, G.E. (1954/5), 'An Account of Excavations in the Cave in Big Covert, Maeshafn, Llanferres', *Trans.Flintshire Historical Soc.*, 141–48. Finds: National Museum of Wales and private hands. Long fissure cave with skeletal remains, a ring and brooches (inc. Figure A7 No.32).

W11: MERLIN'S CAVE SO 556152

Phillips, C.W. (1931), 'Final Report on the Excavations at Merlin's Cave', *P.U.B.S.S.* 4i, 11–33. Finds: Mainly destroyed. Large cave in Wye Valley. Medium sized find assemblage inc. dishes and jars; coins; Ae brooches, bracelets, pins etc.

W12: MINCHIN HOLE SS 55548686

Branigan, K., Dearne, M.J. and Rutter, J.G. (forthcoming), 'Romano-British Occupation of Minchin Hole, Gower', *Arch. Camb.* Finds: Mainly Royal Institute of S. Wales, Swansea. Large high coastal cave on Gower Peninsula. Very important finds from the general area of four hearths. Most important finds a group of very fine bone spoons and late Roman/Dark Age penannular brooches. Significant quantities of fine ware and varied coarse vessel types; numbers of coins; bronze ingot; other bonework; Fe arrowheads and tools.

W13: NANNA'S CAVE SS 14579697

Lacaille, A.D. and Grimes, W.F. (1961), 'The Prehistory of Caldey Part 2', *Arch. Camb.* 110, 30–70. Finds: National Museum of Wales. Square coastal cave on Caldey Island. Small finds assemblage including jars and bowls; one coin; one brooch etc.

CAVE CODE NO. ▶	W8	W9	W10	W11	W12	W13
Date Range (s)	c.75–200	c.75–125	c.75–200	inc c.80–160 c. 270–360	c.140–180 c.280–400+	inc c.140–180 200–400
Fine ware (Sherds)				5	36	1
Coarse Ware (Sherds)				112	740	35+
Coins	?			3	28	1
Glass (Sherds)				X	5	1
Fibulae	1	1	2	1	3	1
Penannular Brooches			1	2	7	
Ae Jewellery/ Toiletry Items			1	9	7	
Ae Working Evidence or Tools					1	
Ae Weighing Items						
Other *Ae* Finds				5	7	1
Fe Weapons					2	
Fe Knives					1	
Fe Tools				1	2	
Other *Fe* Finds				4	38	
Pb Weights						
Other *Pb* Finds				3		
Bone Pins/Fasteners				3	4	2
Other Bone Finds			◡	5	21	
Whetstones				2		
Other Stone Finds		1		4	9+	2
Skeletal Finds (No. of Individuals)		?	6	6		?
Probable Usage	U	B	B	D,B	D,W	0

W14: NANT-Y-GRAIG SJ 00557130

Tankard, E. (1946), 'Notes on Finds in a Limestone Cave at Nant-Y-Graig, Vale of Clwyd', *Arch. Camb.* 99, 119–22. Finds: ?Lost. Rock shelter in small ravine. Sherds of one jar and iron chisel.

W15: OGOF MORFRAN SR 94719377

Davies, M. (1989), 'Cave Archaeology in Southwest Wales', in Ford, T.D. (ed), *Limestones and Caves of Wales*, 77–91. Finds: In private hands. A few fine and coarse sherds and bronze fibula pin from an inaccessible coastal shelter.

W16: OGOF-YR-ESGYRN SN 83781604

Mason, E.J. (1968), 'Ogof-yr-Esgern, Dan-yr-Ogof Caves, Brecknock Excavations 1938–50', *Arch.Camb.* 117, 18–71. Finds: National Museum of Wales, in private hands and Lost. Large cave above modern show cave at source of R. Llynfell. Finds representing at least two phases of activity, the earlier of burial character. Burials with several high quality brooches and unusual penannular. Overall perhaps c.20 vessels including finewares; numbers of coins from both phases; two late Roman silver items; bronzework including steelyard arm and two button and loop fasteners; Fe intaglio ring; bone pins.

W17: OGOF-YR-YCHEN SS 14649692

Ref. as under W13. Finds: Uncertain. Multi-chambered coastal cave on Caldey Island. No details of finds except that they include pottery and the skeletal remains of a child.

W18: PAVILAND CAVE SS 43738588

Williams, A. (1939), 'Prehistoric and Roman Pottery in the Museum of the Royal Institution of S.Wales, Swansea', *Arch. Camb.* 94, 21–9. Finds: Swansea. Coins and sherds of two samian vessels from large but inaccessible coastal cave on Gower Peninsula.

W19: SPRITSAIL TOR DOUBLE ROCK SHELTER SS 42629370

Ref. as under W18. Finds: Swansea. ?Partly quarried-away cave coastal edge cave yielding sherd(s) of one mortarium.

CAVE CODE NO. ▸	W14	W15	W16	W17	W18	W19
Date Range (s)	c.100–300	inc 200–225	c.90–180 c.290–340	?	c.50–100 c.270–310	c.200–400
Fine ware (Sherds)		1	3	?	2	1+
Coarse Ware (Sherds)	1 vessel	1+	92	X		
Coins		2	25		3	
Glass (Sherds)			4			
Fibulae		1	5			
Penannular Brooches			2			
Ae Jewellery/ Toiletry Items			6			
Ae Working Evidence or Tools			1			
Ae Weighing Items			1			
Other *Ae* Finds			3			
Fe Weapons						
Fe Knives						
Fe Tools	1					
Other *Fe* Finds			10			
Pb Weights						
Other *Pb* Finds			1			
Bone Pins/Fasteners			11			
Other Bone Finds			7			
Whetstones						
Other Stone Finds						
Skeletal Finds (No. of Individuals)	?6		40+	1		
Probale Usage	B	H	B,D	B	H	O

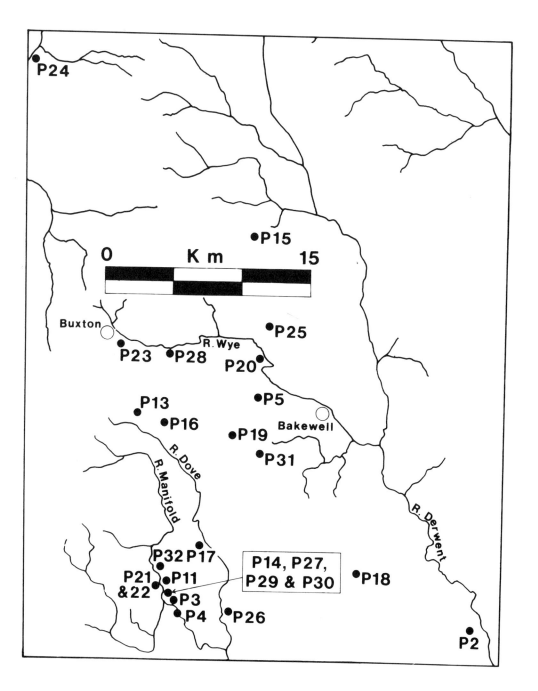

G1 Map of the Peak District showing the location of caves with Romano-British material (see also Figure 4.1).

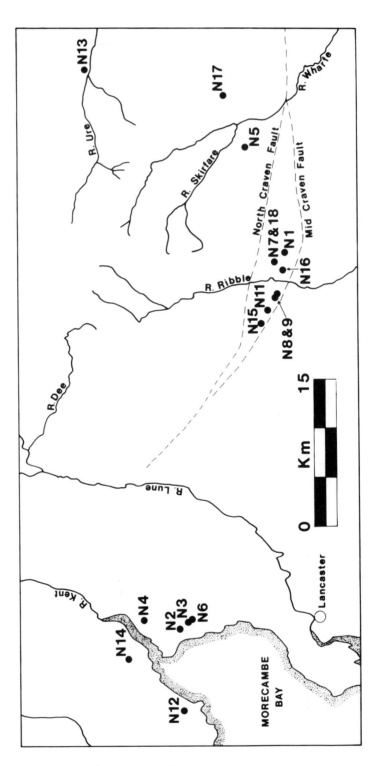

G2   Map of part of Northern England (Settle and Morcambe Bay areas) showing the location of caves with Romano-British material (see also Figure 4.1).

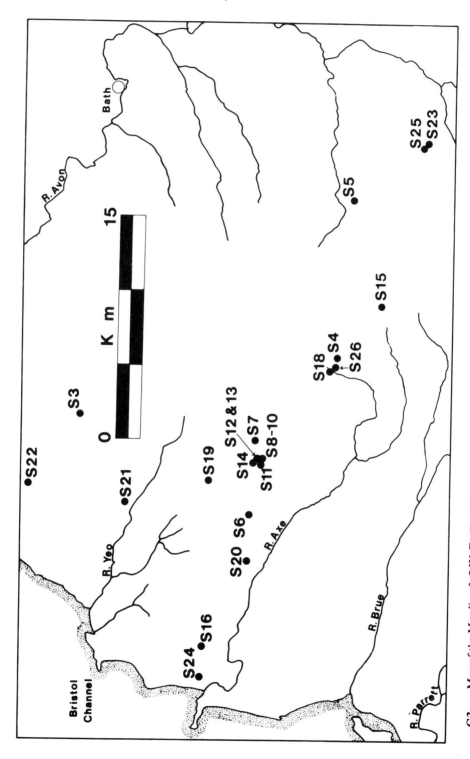

G3   Map of the Mendips & S.W. England showing the location of caves with Romano-British material (see also Figure 4.1).

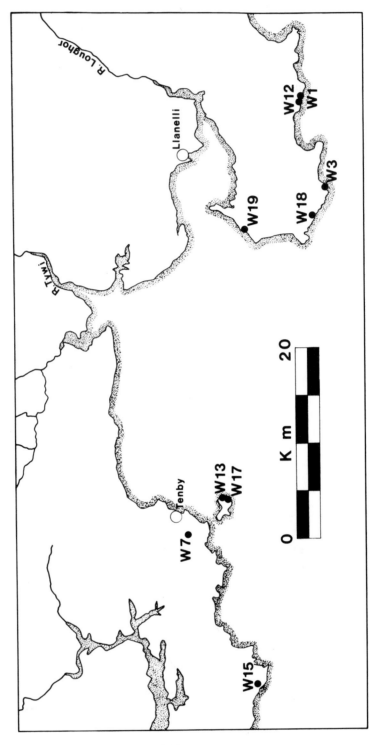

G4 Map of South Wales showing the location of caves with Romano-British material (see also Figure 4.1).